What People Are Saying About
Selling BEYOND Survival

*Lance Coopers book reveals a step-by-step winning sales formula to insure individual and team results. The results are demonstrated by the 100's of companies and thousands of lives who have benefited by **Selling BEYOND Survival**.*

Jack D. Plating, (retired) Executive Vice President & Chief Operating Officer Verizon Wireless

*I was totally **AMAZED** when I reviewed **Selling BEYOND Survival**. It seems like Lance Cooper knew exactly what my sales team was struggling with. He has hit it out of the ball park with this easy to read and understand program designed to help us Coach to a Better Lifestyle. I can't wait to begin using this with my crew. I plan to begin with focus groups of five and work through the book during weekly conference calls.*

Roger D. Anderson, State Manager, Omaha Woodmen Life Insurance Society

*Lance Cooper has discovered the winning formula and put it into understandable form in his very readable **Selling Beyond Survival**. I recommend it and the ideas it promotes. Thank you, Lance, for taking a complex topic and presenting it so simply.*

Jay Conrad Levinson, Author, Guerrilla Marketing, www.gmarketing.com

... the one area where salespeople have complete control - their activities. This powerful, practical, fast-moving book shows you how to get organized and get busy making sales in less time.

Brian Tracy, Author, *The Psychology of Selling*

*If your sales cycle is 90 days or less, read Lance Cooper's **Selling BEYOND Survival**. You'll discover how high-activity sales professionals manage their SALES FUNNEL to achieve their sales and income goals.*
Jill Konrath, Author, SNAP Selling and Selling to Big Companies

*For the first ten years of my professional career, I was directly involved in sales and sales management. IF ONLY I had this resource for myself and my sales personnel, I have no doubt we would have all solved our worst problem: activity management, and had significant increases in our productivity and income. **Selling BEYOND Survival** is, without a doubt, the most comprehensive, yet practical guide to increasing sales productivity that I have ever read. Even if you hire a few "plow horses" instead of "racehorses," this book will provide the structure and motivation they need to be most successful.*
Dr. Larry L. Craft, Author/Developer, The Craft Personality Questionnaire (CPQ)

*In **Selling BEYOND Survival**, Lance Cooper takes you on a wonderful journey to increased selling effectiveness and a better life. In a well-organized, specific, entertaining and readable format he presents a step-by-step plan that can improve the performance of every sales professional. As a bonus, the final part of the book presents an excellent plan for recruiting and coaching a great sales team. I especially enjoyed the emphasis in the book on teaching sales people to make excellent use of their time by identifying and doing those activities that lead to greater sales. It's not the hours we put in our work that matter. It's the work we put in our hours.*
Michael LeBoeuf, Author, *How to Win Customers for Life*

Selling BEYOND Survival is a fabulous guide for salespeople who want to end the struggle and dramatically increase sales. It is loaded with examples and tactics that you can put into action immediately. If you're tired of struggling with your sales processes, this is the book for you. Highly recommended!

Stephanie Chandler, Author, *Own Your Niche: Hype-Free Internet Marketing Tactics to Establish Authority in Your Field and Promote Your Service-Based Business*, www.BusinessInfoGuide.com

Lance Cooper has put together A STEP-BY-STEP WAY for anyone to achieve their sales goals. He starts by walking you through the process of setting goals that get your needs met. Then he takes you by the hand shows you the kinds of activities you need to achieve those goals on a regular basis. It's a logical, common sense, easy-to-grasp system.

Chris Lytle, Author, *The Accidental Salesperson* and *The Accidental Sales Manager*

A great sales person can be terrible as managing the business of selling. Lance Cooper's **Selling BEYOND Survival** provides the missing ingredient that can improve the productivity of even the best of the best.

Al Ries, Author, *War in the Boardroom*

If you call yourself a Sales Professional, you should read **Selling BEYOND Survival**. Successful sales people follow a process and many books have been written about sales techniques. Lance Cooper's book turns the art of selling into an uncomplicated science that focuses on how the right levels of the right activities will lead to success.

Jack Brundige, Director of Sales for U.S. Cellular

Selling BEYOND Survival effectively teaches salespeople to gain better control over their sales results. Lance Cooper's activity management model helps both small business owners and sales professionals consistently achieve their goals. This is a very easy to read book with numerous 'keepers' you can apply immediately.

Dr. Tony Alessandra, Author, *Be Your Own Sales Manager* and *Collaborative Selling*

*What the philosophy of "Moneyball" was to baseball, using the RIGHT players doing the RIGHT processes producing winning success and even World Series Championships, **Selling BEYOND Survival** is to sales! Using the RIGHT levels of the RIGHT activities producing sales success! It's a simple way to look at your belief in a defined process and putting your best efforts towards them to achieve a desired result!*

Greg Karnes, Regional Director, Cellular Sales

Lance Cooper just hit a home run. This comprehensive guide to winning in high-activity sales is one of the best ever written. I just bought this book for my entire sales team and you should too.

Jeb Blount, CEO, Author, *People Buy YOU*, SalesGravy.com

Lance Cooper has a passion to help people, and it comes across in his new book. The diligent reader will read, absorb, and practice the ideas presented. We professionals are always looking for ways to get better.

Ron Willingham, Author, *Integrity Selling for the 21st Century*, and *The Inner Game of Selling*.

I'm sorry to say that most business books on sales say pretty much the same thing. Unfortunately, the results are pretty much the same as well. This book says something quite different. That the system is the solution. That the individual who masters the system will excel, by far, over everyone else. And, that the system Lance Cooper has built and then perfected, is within reach of every single one of us. Great book, Lance Cooper. Great read for the rest of you! Put the System to work!"
Michael E. Gerber, Author, *The E-Myth books*, INC Magazine's "The world's #1 small business guru!"

Lance Cooper has nailed it! Success in sales is engaging in the right activity. He shows you how to shorten your sales cycle and put more money in your pocket faster.
Bill Cates, Author, *Get More Referrals Now!*

Selling BEYOND Survival *cuts straight to the heart of why it's important to understand our strengths and weaknesses, set up long term goals that have real, personal meaning and find the passion in our sales jobs again. Even better, the solution to these problems isn't difficult—in fact, Lance lays it out step by step in a way that anyone can take the system and make it work for them. Ignore the bluster of all the other "business gurus" and use what works in the real world. This is it.*
Jonathan Longnecker, Co-Founder of Kicktastic and FortySeven Media

SELLING
BEYOND SURVIVAL

The Essential System for High-Activity
Sales Professionals

LANCE COOPER

INLIGHT / PUBLISHING
WORDS OF CLARITY

Selling BEYOND Survival: The Essential System for High-Activity Sales Professionals

First Edition: December, 2012

ISBN: 978-0-9886139-0-4

For permissions, training, and speaking engagements
865-599-1115
lcooper@salesmanage.com

Right Levels of Right Activities™

Cover and interior design: Adina Cucicov, Flamingo Designs
Author's photograph: Lorelei Bryan, GentleTouchPortraits.com

Printed in the United States

InLight Publishing (words of clarity)

For more information about related products for high-activity sales professionals go to:

sellingbeyondsurvival.com
salesactivities.com

To the women in my life

My bride, Sheila,
for her tireless acceptance and love
over the last 39 years,
and for her hours of editing and focus on detail.

My mother, Nola,
for her dedication to God and family
and the worlds of love she's given us all
as she works to make "the cash register ring."

My sister, Pam,
for her hard work ethic and perseverance
as a mom, wife, and business manager

My mother-in-law, Smitty,
for her constant prayers and devotion to family
and her constant reminder that "this too shall pass."

CONTENTS

I remember sitting in a Holiday Inn in Knoxville, Tennessee with one of the lobby phones in my hand. I can make outside calls. I have a city directory with enough phone numbers circled for one hour's worth of dials. My palms sweat. The phone seems to weigh 100 lbs.

Yes. I see many salespeople who work hard, but not smart. Their time management slides into activities that are important but not crucial for achieving sales goals. As a result, they do not make enough money to stay employed or pay their bills.

Part II:
Tuning Up Your Engine for Leads and Appointments

In sales, you achieve income goals from each hour of prospecting! Why? Because, whatever closing rate you achieve, continuous prospecting at a right level keeps your income production close to your needs.

PART III:
Managing Elephants, Ants, Rivers, and Activities

It is possible to eat something large over a certain period of time. But, if you stop eating, if you stop the consistent, constant work at it, you will be faced with a time trap—not enough time left to achieve the goal. Usually, you will not catch up.

PART IV:
Managing A Sales Funnel—From Lead To Sale

Great coaches develop a winning spirit of goal achievement among uniquely different human beings. Whether their teams are behind or ahead, competitively outclassed or leading the field, these coaches continually build commitment, hope, and passion into people.

PART V:
Final Thoughts and Tools

The greatest salespeople in the world manage activities with PASS™. Their secret is knowing how to translate their lifestyle goals into daily sales activities.

Introduction

SPINNING WHEELS

I remember sitting in a Holiday Inn in Knoxville, Tennessee with one of the lobby phones in my hand. I can make outside calls. I have a city directory with enough phone numbers circled for one hour's worth of dials. My palms sweat. The phone seems to weigh 100 lbs. Perspiration, heart beats, pulse pounding. People in the hotel walk by—some of them are employees. Their eyeballs seem to expand and fix on me sitting in their hotel, and using their phone, as stress causes me to hallucinate.

Back home I have a letter saying the bank will auction off my house on a certain date at the courthouse steps. People I don't know dance up and down the steps waiting for a chance to take my home. My bride and my young sons are unaware ... that I have to make a sale. They're eating breakfast before going off to school.

▼ ▼ ▼

Are you a professional, high-activity sales rep—someone who closes new sales each day, week, or month? Someone who does this to meet a quota or commission level? Is the sales cycle for most of your sales ninety days or less? Are you stalled at a performance level below or near financial survival? Do you see wild swings in sales closings from month to month? Do you eat well some months and then starve during others? Does the bank want to auction off your home?

If so, I want to help YOU.

For almost thirty years, I have trained and coached thousands of high-activity sales reps and their leaders with great results. During that time I've helped them develop sales plans, activity management processes, and face-to-face skills. Many of my students have made thousands of dollars more per sales period as a result of my training. Even more importantly, the principles and advice I've given has helped them improve their lives away from the job. I love to get those calls and emails.

A SALES SCIENCE: ACTIVITY MANAGEMENT

So, why write a book. Why this book? Because I want to help you learn a science that isn't written about very often, but will have a dramatic effect on your sales, confidence, and professionalism. I want this book to help you learn how to manage the sales activities that will help you achieve your sales and income goals. I want to teach you how to do the *Right Levels of the Right Activities.*™ I want to teach you about a science that well-trained, high-activity sales professionals recognize as Activity Management.

Every day millions of small business owners, consultants, entrepreneurs, service or product providers put on their marketing hats and sales shoes. Some of them know to use a prospect list. Others need to look up the word prospect. These sales professionals socialize at chamber of commerce meetings and show up at community clubs and association meetings. But most don't know how to manage the activities that will help them achieve sale goals. They don't know what levels of specific activities will keep them on track.

THE SIMPLE SALES PROCESS OF HIGH-ACTIVITY SALES PROFESSIONALS

Years ago, Michael Gerber helped entrepreneurs discover the world of processes and the franchise prototype through his book, *The E-Myth*. He explains, "Once having completed his Prototype, the franchisor turned to the franchisee and says, 'Let me show you how it works.'" And, work it does. The system runs the business, the people run the system. To entrepreneurs who read Michael's book, this simple understanding between system and business and people and system explains **how to make what they love work by the numbers by capturing results through organized and repeatable methods—step-by-step processes.**

I want to reveal the activity management system of a, high-activity, sales professional. I want to show you its processes, tools, and skills. I want you to know how to plan your sales goal achievement by steps and numbers. I also want you to know that achievement will still depend upon your commitment, passion, and hope in the journey. It will still depend upon customer satisfaction and great service. But, I don't want you to start with a smile only to lose hope because no one taught you what was in this book. I want you to be smart about high-activity sales and the system that brings results.

When you sell, you operate the sales engine of a business that has control and output rules—systematic rules. You can create. You can innovate. You can still love what you do. You can still show passion toward your products and services, but you know to follow the rules. If you do not follow rules within an activity management system, the business of sales does not bring its allotment of cash to the enterprise. Cash flow sputters with unmanageable highs and lows as prospects, appointments, and other inputs of the sales engine operate at danger levels. Throwing new reps and entrepreneurs into sales is like giving an airplane and its passengers to a new pilot who hasn't been taught how to fly with instrumentation controls. He's loved planes since his youth, but at night he flies blind relying on instinct without a basic understanding of where he is along the path to his destination. Worse than that, others depend on him—co-workers, vendors, and a business of people.

AN EMPOWERING RELATIONSHIP BETWEEN ACTIVITY AND RESULTS

See people—find out their needs—present solutions—make sales. Simple. Just go out and make it happen. Throw enough mud on the wall until some of it sticks. Put a new rep in the field and say "sic 'em!" Right? Wrong. That's a recipe for unnecessary turnover, hurt lives, and cash flow disaster.

You can have a 100% closing rate and go out of business. How? Make one sale per month when you need five to pay the bills and have enough left over to buy groceries.

You can fill your calendar with appointments, close every sale, and lose your sales position. Why? You did not have enough 1st appointments and presentations with new potential prospects. Each month your sales were below budget. You were then fired.

You can work harder than other salespeople, put in more hours, be an honest person, have a great product, and only make enough money to barely survive. How? You did not manage to do the "Right Levels of the Right Activities.™"

I want to empower you by helping you learn about the relationship between activity and results. When my students learn this system, they learn to work smart and use their time to make more sales. Their activities lead to results.

THIS BOOK'S DESIGNED FOR YOU

I want to pull at the fabric of your heart. I want to teach you a system that will help you, but I don't want the system to steal your individuality, creativity, or freedom. I want you to love what I'm teaching and to see that discipline and a right road will keep you safe and provide a place where your creativity can flourish. I do not want you traveling the dangerous grounds of unrestrained action.

There are four parts to the book. Each part is comprised of seven sections and ends with meaning and purpose and action steps. It's important to read and experience these in sequence, as each part builds on the last. You can self-customize it to your circumstances as you learn.

GROWING AND LEARNING AS YOU READ

I want to increase your understanding so that you make positive actionable changes to your activity. So, please write in this book, on it, and around it. Highlight it. Apply the sections to your sales and your industry. Use scratch paper. Design YOUR system. When you see an action or a better way to use your time, begin those actions at once. Don't wait until you finish the book.

Show your notes and planning to others you trust for their counsel. Bounce the book's ideas off their reflections. Challenge its concepts. Do not do what it says with a blind obedience. Test it. Make adjustments as your grow and learn.

INITIAL DECISIONS YOU MAKE

When you work through the sections around goals and planning, make conservative estimates. If you have a family, get your spouse involved in deciding income requirements. Talk to sales managers—even those in other industries. Get their observations and industry experience regarding ratios and best practice. Do this. Many of you will have no prior history to guide your decisions toward appropriate activity levels. I will give you some thoughts about these, but you must test these for yourself. Find out what's true by using the ideas about tracking.

In some cases, some of you will work in industries with well thought out activity management ratios. Always start with these. This book will reinforce the training you receive there and the activity rules you learn. It will help you build confidence. It will be a great outside resource for you as your strengthen this part of your professionalism.

FINALLY—EVOLVE TOWARD WHAT'S RIGHT!

I love high-activity sales professionals and I appreciate the confidence you've displayed in purchasing and reading this book. I also applaud your desire for self-development and coaching.

I expect you will learn from me and from others who turn back and write for those in their footprints. Look over the books and the websites of the experts who have endorsed this book. Perhaps you will find your next area for improvement from among them. Please tell me your thoughts as well. Tell me other ways to think and learn about time management and productivity in sales. I've drawn my pictures. Show me yours. Tell me your stories.

Get better. I believe you can. If I can make mistakes and learn from them, you can as well.

Lance

PART I

GOALS AND DIRECTION FOR HIGH-ACTIVITY SALES PROFESSIONALS

Never mistake activity for achievement.
JOHN WOODEN

Chapter 1

SMART ACTIVITY

What do great salespeople do with their selling time in a week? **Smart activity.** They realize that **activity leads to results, and smart activity leads to greatness.**

Does that mean that some salespeople miss what's smart? Yes. I see many salespeople who work hard, but not smart. Their time management slides into activities that are important but not crucial for achieving sales goals. As a result, they do not make enough money to stay employed or pay their bills. Or, they do not get far enough ahead to help themselves or their families enjoy a better lifestyle. They produce at survival levels.

What does this look like?

Picture three reps working hard but not smart. One prepares beautiful proposals with great detail and organization. Another spends too much time with unqualified prospects. The third rep either does not discover customer needs strong enough to justify preparing a proposal or he does not present or follow up on proposals he issues. The proposals are pretty, the meetings are held, the presentations occur, the needs are found. However, these three salespeople do not get enough of the right activities done in a month to achieve their goals.

They spin their wheels just above a road paved with smart activity.

Examples are all around us. A talkative sales rep spends more time than is necessary in sales and customer service calls. Another does not schedule the right amount of first appointments with new prospects. And neither finds enough new prospects each month to prosper. They work hard. But, they do not know how many presentations to do or quotes to issue to reach their goals. They do not know how many first appointments it takes to issue the right number of quotes. They do not know how many new prospects must be found each and every month.

They do not know.

I want you to know.

I want you and those you provide for to win the prizes, the trips, the lifestyle.

Let's put those wheels on the ground and GO!

PRODUCTIVE STRESS IN A HIGH-ACTIVITY SALES WORLD

It's the first of the month for high-activity sales professionals. For the next 28-31 working days, entrepreneurs, small business owners, and salespeople in various markets will strive to close a certain number of sales. They sprint to the finish line at the end of the month racing for sales results ahead of budget or on goal. They will do this to survive or prosper, and then start the process over again the very next month.

Some high-activity sales professionals close sales every day. Others close them at a weekly or monthly rate. For salespeople in this excited world of hyper-activity, the sales cycle from finding prospects to closing sales is 90 days or less. Occasionally, a few sales take longer that 90 days, but they are the exception and not the rule.

During each week, high-activity professionals cram a lot of prospecting and face-to-face selling activity into each sales day. Analysis and paperwork is minimized in this kind of environment. Professionals in this fast-paced environment strive to maximize time spent in front of prospective customers or fight to get in front of them.

Proposals are kept simple by using the same basic outline, customized with the prospect name, amount, and the services or products quoted. High-activity salespeople deliver face-to-face product or service quotes in 3- to 60-minute presentations, and usually to one or possibly two decision makers. They find new customers or clients each month.

STRESS AND ANXIETY

For many, this month and those before it were full of stress and anxiety stemming from cash flow swings and inconsistent sales. Sometimes delivering the products and services sold gets in the way of making enough new sales, and hard work does not produce appropriate sales and income levels. The lack of results creates uncertainty about where to focus for important change that would make sales and cash flow become more predictable—even steady or constant.

The best make it work. Somehow, they do it, but they can't seem to teach what works. Others survive, but just barely. They hang on near survival, either at quota or at income rates that sustain only the bare necessities of life: food, lodging, automobile, phone, clothing, etc. The rest fall away quickly to be replaced by the next generation of new reps. Very few of them have a model for effective time management in this high-activity selling world that keeps the right activities at the right levels.

ERIC—"THE UNRESTRAINED HORSE"

Managing time at one extreme is Eric, a salesman I've coached. When I watch him in action, he does work hard—very hard. You might say he is impulsive, goal-oriented, and scattered. He is also the breadwinner in the family. His wife works part-time and helps with paying the insurance bill.

Eric doesn't even have a to-do list. He just reacts. He reacts with prospects, appointments, and with end-of-the-month paperwork. Eric really is a gifted salesperson when face-to-face. He can close sales, but only up to a certain plateau because he runs out of time.

His lack of knowledge about how to prioritize and manage sales activities leads him into too few prospects, appointments and quotes to reach or increase his sales goals.

In every group of salespeople, a few operate like Eric. Do you? I'm sure you have a to-do list, but are your sales consistently above budget needs? Do you know how to prioritize the most necessary activities, the ones that lead to enough sales each month? Do you know how to make yourself more efficient and effective with time?

Eric needs to find new prospects and sell a certain amount of business each and every month. He doesn't need big hits, but bread and butter business from a certain amount of widgets or revenue sold. He needs to stay focused on doing enough of the right activities that lead directly to commissionable income.

He needs a new activity process. Do you?

MARIA—"THE MOTHER OF ALL"

Some high-activity salespeople like recognition. Maria does. She likes it a lot. She also enjoys taking care of her customers. Each day I see her work as if she has an obligation to satisfy every need or request from her customers.

She often gets to the end of the month exhausted and short of her sales goal. Maria, like Eric, is stalled at a plateau she cannot seem to rise above. Her income stays about the same, and it's not high enough to get ahead of her basic needs.

On the other hand, customers love Maria and all she does to help them. It seems to her that she could do more for them, and she tries. She works off endless lists of return phone calls, meetings, follow-up cards, scheduled lunches, and customer-focused events. Her meetings and phone calls take a lot of time and she strives to get the most out of every one of them. Sometimes, because of their duration, she finds herself late for other appointments.

Even with her dedicated servant heart, at the end of each month the paychecks don't rise. She finds it difficult to continue prospecting for new customers because existing customer needs take so much time and the rewards aren't high enough.

Maria wonders why things are different from her new rep days when she ran hard at finding new customers and sales seemed to rise very quickly. Today, she works without the same excitement or enthusiasm. She tries to hide this, but she just feels tired and her early rep confidence is replaced by a dogged approach to the day.

She knows something needs to change and it's probably her. She just doesn't know what will help her get higher sales results along with great customer satisfaction. She needs help.

JACKSON—"THE THINKING GURU"

When you meet Jackson and watch him use time and resources, it's easy to see his intelligence. He understands efficiencies and how to make time for the things that excite his intellect. For example, he enjoys putting together the approach to each sale, especially the proposals and research behind each customer solution. He loves the analytical side of a sale.

Very few salespeople can match Jackson's understanding of product features and how to analyze customer situations. That's why you see other salespeople come to him for advice, which he freely gives. And yet, while he sometimes networks into and makes a big sale, he misses the appointment levels necessary to bring in the smaller "bread and butter sales" that require fewer steps and less mind work.

Jackson is really good at understanding effective time management as it relates to prioritizing tasks and minimizing travel. When he tries to analyze his sales levels and how to get them to new heights, he focuses first on the inadequate support staff. He wants someone else to do the grunt work: administrative, boring work not related to analysis and systematic problem solving or large ideas. While this is an important factor, it is not the factor most hindering his sales goal achievement.

Jackson gets lost in the big deals and the analysis. He likes them. He likes to wrap his mind around them. His "big deal-itis" also lures him into other new company areas requiring analysis. Without really understanding his own tendencies, Jackson uses time for non-critical activities throughout each sales period. He never seems to get the most important sales activities to levels necessary for sales goal achievement at the highest level.

Giving him support staff would not change his tendencies. He would still find his mind lured into those areas that require strategic thought and complex processes. Without an understanding of the impact on his income, Jackson's interest in areas outside of critical selling activities would keep his income down to survival. He would not thrive.

Jackson, Maria, and Eric need a system that helps them get the most important sales activities at a high enough volume for sales and income goal achievement. They need a system that helps them analyze and make changes in their habits—habits related to sales skills and self-management.

JESSICA—"THE LEARNING PROFESSIONAL"

We first see Jessica at a recruiting fair. She's just out of college, doesn't know anything about sales, but wants to make a new life for herself.

Jessica's family life growing up was sometimes hard and sacrificial. Her mother raised two children as a single mom on a limited income. To pitch in some dollars, Jessica learned to work early in her life with a part-time job during high school. She gave up social status and friendships to help the household. During this formative time in her life, Jessica watched her mom work 8 to 5 as an executive secretary doing the best she could on a limited income.

Today, Jessica wants something different and she is willing to do whatever she can to make it happen. She fills out an application, makes it through the interviews, and signs on as a brand new sales rep.

In the next 6 months, Jessica rises to the top of her sales team and three years later still continues among high achievers in the company. How? What made the difference? Talent? Intelligence? Well, actually ... no. In interviews and testing, she had an average intelligence and moderate rankings as a sales match with her position.

> Jackson, Maria, and Eric need a system that helps them get the most important sales activities at a high enough volume for sales and income goal achievement.

Then, what was it?

It had much to do with internal drive and desire ... and a simple focus given by her sales manager in a new activity management system provided for first year reps.

A STEP FORWARD

Amazed at Jessica's performance, Eric broke through to higher sales performance. He learned to change a few actions in his daily routine into smarter activities.

Why did Eric change his approach? His wife was pregnant and leaving the work force. The need to be the sole breadwinner in his family caused him to consider new ways to improve. He just HAD TO move to higher commissions.

As a veteran on the team, it had been difficult to watch Jessica's fast start and continued rise to high performance. It was easy to explain her success as beginner's luck for the first few months. However, as she kept on finding and selling new customers, this explanation did not fit her sustained results. Eric decided to talk with her about it. Jessica's response was straightforward and easy to understand. "When I began my sales career, I knew one thing. I didn't want to just get by—to exist. I wanted more."

Eric wasn't buying that as the explanation.

"I want that, too. Who doesn't?"

What Jessica said next floored him and she spoke the words without pride or undue emotion. "Eric, I just did what they told me. I didn't know anything else to do."

With her as an example of the new coaching and activity management system, Eric went to his sales manager and asked to be included. What he learned revolutionized his approach to activity management. It changed his life. It improved the standard of living for his family.

▼ ▼ ▼

As you read this book, I want you to learn to use the process that made Jessica successful and transformed Eric's performance. The SalesActivities System they used contains a step-by-step process with simple tools and skills. I hope you find inspiration in learning how to use it for your benefit. The SalesActivities system will help you do the *Right Levels of the Right Activities.*™ It will help you manage the sales activities necessary to achieve your income goals.

Now, what's a process?

Chapter 2

A BRICK-BUILDING SALES PROCESS

High-activity sales professionals like Eric and Jessica work in a short sales cycle. Sales for them usually occur after one or two appointments held with a prospect in less than 90 days. Wireless  sales reps, IT and general business consultants, financial advisors, sales trainers, and mortgage brokers are a few sales types that experience this fast-paced selling environment. In some high-paced industries, like wireless (or cellular phones), reps close several sales a day.

Even commercial realtors see decisions occur within 90 days from finding an opportunity (someone who wants to list their property) to getting the listing (a realtor's first sale). While the actual sale or leasing of the property may take months or even years, prospects for signed listing agreements make quick decisions when they want a professional to represent them.

PROCESS

We define a process as a step-by-step series of actions leading to a desired result. For example, if I want to get to the other side of a room of trainees, I've got a choice. I can travel around various tables to get to my desired end point. Or, I can walk up to and then climb over the tables to arrive at the other side of the room. Or, I can go outside by exiting through a window, walk to the hotel entrance and into the training room, and again arrive at my destination. One of these routes is a smarter path. The others are not. All are effective at getting me to my destination, but of unequal efficiency.

BUILDING BRICK WALLS

I've asked many sales teams the following question, "What would we do, if we, as novice brick builders, had to build a brick wall 100 feet long and 4 feet high in 31 days and then build another? What would we do first, second, etc.?"

Most teams say, "Hire a brick-builder" or, "Get the tools together." The problem is we're novices and we do not know what the tools are, where to put them, and what is most efficient to do first.

I also hear, "Figure out how many bricks per hour and day." That's because while the end-result is a brick wall, we need to make progress at a steady rate: X number of bricks laid per hour, day, and week. If we vary in consistent work output, we will not have enough days for the bricks we have left to lay.

What tools do we need? "Trowel, shovel, wheelbarrow, ..."

Where do we put them? How can we minimize travel back and forth to the wall for efficiency and to lay the maximum amount of bricks? Remember, we have to finish the wall in 31 days. Then, we have to start over again.

BUILDING MONTHLY SALES

High-activity sales works like building brick walls. Maybe we must sell 100 widgets per month. Every month we pursue a certain number of sales in a 31-day time period. We work to make steady progress in units sold or revenue sold so we can be halfway to our goal by the midpoint of each month. We've got to finish the wall (get a certain amount of revenue or units sold) in 31 days, and then start over. We don't want to get toward the end of the month with fewer days available than what we need to reach our income goals.

When building brick walls, we mix our mortar, mud our bricks, and then lay them. These are important brick-building activities. Typical activities in our sales process include finding prospects, phoning to set appointments, holding appointments (first appointments and follow up calls), presenting solutions and quotes, asking for the business, and completing necessary new customer paperwork.

If installation is involved, we also have to provide the product or service, or communicate with those who will. While delivery or installation occurs for previous sales, keeping a steady stream of prospective customers helps sales remain at a consistent level above minimum requirements or near our income needs.

Often this simple sales process—appointment, presentation, and necessary follow up—requires convincing one decision maker who wants a need filled in a short amount of time. Larger sales that take longer to close and that require convincing multiple decision makers are not the norm.

High-activity sales professionals usually earn most of their income from making average size sales that require a minimum of appointments and complexity. It's this basic "bread and butter" sale that feeds the family and keeps cash flowing. For these "normal" sales, *the most important (critical) activities within a sales process are*:

1. **Finding new prospects.**
2. **Holding first appointments.**
3. **Conducting closing presentations (presenting quotes).**

As my business partner, Steve Suggs, has often said, *"A great salesperson spends a majority of available working hours either in front of prospects or fighting to get in front of them."*

SALES CYCLE

A high-activity sales process implies quicker decisions and multiple sales in a simple selling cycle to reach quota or personal goal achievement. As the type of sale changes from simple to complex, the sales cycle lengthens to 90 days or beyond to get a buying decision. Then, more strategic thinking and positioning must occur to decide the next action that gets the business. A high-activity world can have a few complex sales sprinkled among the normal fast cycle ones.

The high-activity sale usually closes within the 90-day window (the high-activity sales cycle). Cash flow begins and perhaps completes itself for each sale in this same period. Sales professionals operating in this sales cycle make multiple sales in a day, week, or month. The best are goal-oriented, confident, and like to get a lot done in a short amount of time. But that's not all.

> *Achieving high monthly sales or revenue, profit or income requires an efficient use of time that brings most important or critical sales activities to elevated levels.*

Achieving high monthly sales or revenue, profit or income requires an efficient use of time that brings most important or critical sales activities to elevated levels. The right activity management keeps salespeople in front of *enough* new potential customers or clients per selling period.

ERIC, MARIA, AND JACKSON

For different reasons, these three did not use time well. They did not get enough critical selling activities accomplished to stay on track to meet their goals. They missed doing enough of the critical sales activities each week to remain consistent in prospects found, appointments set and held, and deals closed.

▼ ▼ ▼

Before he changed his habits, Eric lost track of what to do next, especially with hot prospects. He worked hard, but actually forgot about deals-in-progress until it was too late to follow up. On the positive side, some of his customers loved him because he meant well and handled their needs well when he was with them.

Other prospects, especially those with greater potential and more complex needs, were disappointed with Eric's lack of promise fulfillment. They avoided him when he finally remembered to call them back. At times, he showed up without an appointment, smiling and willing to help, but unannounced. He came across as an interruption to employees who worked for accounts that valued efficiency and accountability. They asked that he not call on them again.

Eric did not plan his days or appointments well. He carried no working prospect or deals-in-progress list and scheduled appointments without much regard for geography or travel time. He also had no idea of the number of quotes he made each month. He just reacted, cold-called for business, and wrote down the names of businesses on trucks that passed by, and worked hard.

Needless to say, Eric most always found himself behind at mid-month and in a scurry to catch up before the days were gone. Only rarely did he exceed his normal sales level, until his breakthrough.

▼ ▼ ▼

Maria's day, while altogether different, produced the same results. She did not forget customer needs or promises and worked diligently at to-do lists. Her appointments were generally long ones and she made sure to treat each person in the account with respect and attention—even lobby receptionists whom she knew by name.

High-energy executives with little time to waste passed her off to support staff. Maria then spent inordinate amounts of time socializing with them and attending to their needs. She frequently attended installation of her products even though she really wasn't needed and had no role to play.

At some point during the month, Maria, like Eric, lost track of her sales goal progress. If it were not for the sales meetings her manager held, she would not know her actual sales versus goal. However, the meetings did not help her productivity. They just reminded her how far she was behind meeting her budget numbers.

▼ ▼ ▼

Where's Jackson? Studying the competition. Reviewing the prospect's web site. Putting together spreadsheets. Thinking about new initiatives.

And relative to goal? He's behind. But, he's got a lot working. He has a bunch of sales-in-progress. However, he gets himself side tracked by interesting new alignments and problems in the organization. His active mind, with nothing to keep it harnessed into important sales activities, wanders away from critical sales activities.

The large accounts love him. At times, this translates into a great month, which is often followed by famine. Consistency does not define him. Jackson's wife keeps hearing about the big deals in the works, but only sees enough income to feel secure once every 3 or 4 months.

Without someone or a process to focus him, Jackson's activity levels suffer when his strength of intellect pulls him into activities not aligned with necessary sales levels. He needs to stay on pace with the right amount of critical sales activities. To survive in a fast-paced sales environment, he needs to change soon—very soon.

BACK TO BRICKS

Brick masons keep the bricks moving one at a time, a certain amount each day to get the wall up by the end of the month. High-activity sales professionals do the same with a steady stream of prospects, appointments, quotes, and sales. They are consistent, ever moving, with the right amount of each activity to yield enough meetings with qualified prospects to result in the right amount of closed sales every 31 days.

DAILY, WEEKLY, OR MONTHLY SALES LEVELS

Depending on business needs, high-activity salespeople make three to six sales per day, week, or month to achieve their goals. Their skills are needed in these service and product sales arenas: insurance, home and commercial security systems, consultants, financial services, water purification, wireless/cellular, telecom, home improvement, repair and remodelers, residential and small commercial real estate, specialty medical equipment, landscape design, advertising, marketing, mortgage loan officers, specialty retail, and many others.

Certainly, complex sales occur in these industries. However, bread and butter sales usually close within a 90-day period.

REFERRAL STRENGTH

When the best high-activity sales professionals bring in enough new sales each month, they do so with great customer satisfaction that protects the brand of the business. They do this because they deliver value. As an added bonus, their referrals increase. Customers want to help them. Appointment setting is easier. Their closing rates go up.

A natural market helps a new sales rep progress at a faster rate in the beginning. A natural market contains those people with whom the new sales rep already has a relationship and who might have a reasonable need for the product or service represented. Later as a seasoned salesperson, referral strength improves activity ratios within the high-activity sales process. It improves efficiencies and productivity for all concerned: sales reps, customers, installers, and business owners.

Chapter 3

SALES GOALS THAT CHANGE YOUR LIFE

Before we focus on *Right Levels of Right Activities*™, we need to start at the beginning with the right sales goal. What's really important? Why this sales goal and not that one?

Many entrepreneurs and high-activity sales professionals work out of survival. They do not think to organize activities to accomplish what it takes for a better way of life, so they end up managing sales activities that provide for survival needs (mortgage payment, food, minimum debt payment, etc.) and possibly failure. Salespeople automatically default to efforts that keep them eating, sleeping, communicating, and traveling. As a result, work gets designed for mediocrity levels not lifestyle and not greatness.

Even those who work at higher aspirations may find themselves without specifics. In some cases, top salespeople do not pay attention to future requirements. They don't know where their money goes. They do not have a plan leading to a better lifestyle and future. They chase more money, greater recognition, or advancement without an eye on what lies ahead. Even as their achievement progresses, their quality of life gets worse with greater  debt, credit card payments, and other obligations without adequate resources in savings. The financial stress and burden grows larger on them and their family.

Some high-activity sales reps do what's expected. Rather than think for themselves, they do their duty. While commendable as a character trait, this behavior can cause a lack of self-discipline toward the fiscal reality of their personal needs. The goal given them by their sales manager may be too small for their own survival or future realities. Usually, sales budgets, sales goals, and resulting incomes do not reflect YOUR needs. They represent the COMPANY's needs. I watch sales reps get a high-five on recognition day and then have to borrow money to pay for repairs to their roof.

If any of this happens to you, how do you change? How do you become more mature in your use of money and in setting goals that affect your future and what your situation demands?

FIRST STEP

When you design a sales goal, look at your income needs for a better lifestyle. Do this by adding together income required to take care of survival needs and lifestyle needs.

To begin, let's start with adding together all your budget numbers for survival: food, rent or mortgage, gas, etc. Add up monthly obligations that you must pay just to stay even and keep yourself or your family eating, sleeping, communicating, and traveling. And let's keep the lenders and government (taxes) away from our doors. Follow the example shown below by plugging in your own numbers. If I haven't thought of something that you consider survival, just add the category into the example.

Survival Example (monthly):

Mortgage payment (or rent payment) = 1600.00
Food = 1000.00
Car payment = 450.00
Car insurance = 100.00
Fuel = 350.00
Credit card payment = 250.00
Utilities = 250.00
Cell phone = 100.00
Taxes = ?
Survival Total = 4100.00 + taxes per month

SECOND STEP

Determine next what amount of monthly income you need for a better lifestyle in the future. Add up the amount of monthly income you need for things like these: debt reduction, college savings, down payment for a house, home repairs/improvement, etc. Be conservative as you estimate the specific amount of income you will need over the next 12 months for each area. Then turn each into a monthly income requirement.

Better Lifestyle Example (monthly)

New roof at a cost of $7,200 (7200.00 ÷ 12) = 600.00
Additional savings of $12,000 (12000.00 ÷ 12) = 1000.00
College saving plan for teenage son: this year's part of the plan equals $12,000 (12000.00 ÷ 12) = 1000.00
Pay down credit card balance an additional $6000.00 = 500.00
Better Lifestyle Total = 3100.00 per month

After doing the above steps, add your monthly survival and lifestyle needs together for a total necessary income. Finally, turn this income goal into a sales goal as you think about base pay and commissions.

Survival + Better Lifestyle

Survival Total = 4100.00
Better Lifestyle Total = 3100.00
Survival + Lifestyle Income = $7200.00 + taxes (amount paid for Federal and State Income Tax) per month

Doing Survival/Lifestyle goal planning increases your achievement drive and the inspiration behind your sales goal. It provides the WHY behind the numbers and puts reality and desire into sales goal achievement. You now work for a better way of life, a life of higher quality, and your sales goal becomes the pathway to this future state.

As your inspiration increases, you improve perseverance, accountability, and performance. With a greater understanding of activity management, you can change the levels of critical sales activities to build enough sales for a better lifestyle.

ERIC'S TRANSFORMATION

The change for Eric occurred when his sales manager helped him see his situation by the numbers. Eric wanted his wife, Sarah, at home, and she wanted to be there to care for their kids. However, he operated at activity levels inconsistent with the sales goal achievement he needed to bring her out of her office job. His income and hers kept them just above survival. Their young kids got daycare—not mom. She was forced to remain employed.

At his present activity level, Eric did work hard. But his prospecting and quoting activities were insufficient. His income from commissions when added to Sarah's, produced a household income that was barely above what they needed to pay the bills.

The first ah-ah for Eric occurred when he said, "I've got to earn $10,000 per month." And then he paused, his eyes widened and he exclaimed, "I've got to change my appointments and quote levels to bring Sarah home. I've got to. I've got to close more sales!"

Eric needed a coach to see beyond survival and to see his true income goal. He needed a coach to help him see what he must change—how to manage his activities with more efficiency. He especially needed a coach to help him through the difficulties of change. Could he do it? Would the new methods be effective? Could he break old habits?

Eric had to change. He had to.

Do you have to?

JESSICA'S DRIVE

Remember Jessica's drive? Her HAD TO? Where did it come from? How was it affected by working during high school and by reflecting on her mother's sacrifice? How did seeing this change her behavior and make her become more specific with what she did with her money and how much she earned? How did this affect her coachability as a new rep?

Unharnessed drive in new and old reps can lead to mediocre results. If not channeled toward important sales activities, reps can work hard but not smart. It can lead to bad habits. Enough failure over time can lead to resignation and then disappointment with life. But not for Jessica. From the beginning of her employment, her sales manager helped her understand the reality of her goals and the activities required to achieve them. She started out on the right track—one that helped her perform as a high achiever right from the start.

Interestingly, many new reps start out on a good road just like Jessica did. You can see their unadulterated and pristine attitude bringing success to their initial steps. Hope empowers them. Sometime later their great start begins to fade. They fall in production. Their drive diminishes. Why?

Too often, new reps bog down as their initial excitement wears off. What are the top reasons? For some, their hearts are not driven to accomplish meaningful goals and as they leave the limelight focused on them as new reps, their production falls. Others begin to listen to poor or mediocre performance talk from those around them who have stopped growing. As they listen and believe the negative discussions, the new reps lose their achievement drive. Jessica didn't listen. She couldn't. She had to grow.

Even if motivation continues and is sustained by longer-lasting motivators, a rep can still begin to slide into inefficient time usage habits. You might ask, "How does this happen?" The bad habits creep into and over the day until a new rep is overwhelmed with important but less than critical demands relative to sales production. Without realizing it, a rep begins to major in minor activities, and the activities driving sales performance drop to unproductive levels.

The emerging inefficiencies can be as simple as not paying attention to the distance between appointments. Doing necessary paperwork, attending meetings, taking coffee breaks, and talking with co-workers begin to climb over a day like a Kudzu vine, smothering essential sales tasks. Even customer service can eliminate time for critical selling activities.

Jessica really didn't experience this time management trap of inefficiencies. She didn't because someone guided her through her ramp up and first critical selling year. While she did notice that other reps started well but then fell off, she was too busy with prospecting, appointments, and quoting activities to understand why. As she developed relationships with other top performers, her can-do attitude propelled her into making progress toward important achievements and lifestyle development. While it is important to make this journey alone, her sales manager's activity system and association with top performers kept her momentum strong.

COMPETITION AND RECOGNITION—BEING IN THE TOP

While putting numbers on paper is necessary to understand your fiscal responsibilities, this may not provide the motivation you require, especially if you have an overdeveloped competitive spirit or drive for recognition. Sales often attracts those personalities who like to define themselves through winning contests. If you believe success lies in being victorious among your peers, then survival and lifestyle goals may not be enough for your internal motivation. You may need to be at or near the top.

If you love to win competitions or enjoy gaining recognition for your performance, find out what the top people in your company, marketplace, or industry achieve. Investigate and quantify their monthly sales and income levels. Find out *exactly* what it takes to be the best or at the top.

Once you know the monthly income levels of top performers and their corresponding sales levels, you can continue learning with us about what it takes to achieve these levels through the *Right Levels of Right Activities.* ™

MOVING ON WITHOUT JUDGMENT

Here's something I believe. *Don't look back.*

Most of you are reading this book to learn skills and attitudes for greater income production. To do so will require maximum attention on your own stuff and a willingness to make mistakes as you plow new ground. Ruminating on the past will slow you down. *Don't look back.*

Don't focus on your failures. Learn from them and then forget them. Look ahead with new skills and new attitudes you have learned and absorbed from your people and influencers that believe in the new ways and the levels of income production associated with them. *Don't look back.*

Allow dissatisfaction with old values to occur as new values occur to you. What do I mean when I say "old values?" I mean the activities you used to value like previous prospecting methods, monthly appointment and quoting levels, closing ratios, and monthly sales numbers. Especially look for new values in activity management. Look for new ways to manage your use of time and pay attention to which activities you assign to the amount of time available. Look for new sales processes, tools and skills that save time, increase sales, and get referrals.

Learn from those you admire because they are more successful than you. Ask for help. Gravitate toward higher performers—toward those who think and act in ways that produce greater sales. As you move on with them, you won't look back. You will move on without judging yourself. Let condemnation and failure stay on the road behind you. Instead move on with a desire to learn and grow.

Look ahead. You can get better. You can be better. You can.

Chapter 4

RIGHT LEVELS OF RIGHT ACTIVITIES™

HIGH-ACTIVITY

Many pure analytic people do not work fast because of their genetic strength in detail and perhaps method. Others work slowly, not because of the brain or genetics, but because of a character issue like laziness. Whatever the reason, some people don't cram a lot of activity, especially social connectivity and face-to-face activity, into each day or week.

But certain industries require action-oriented salespeople focused on doing with minimal thinking. In those selling cultures, lots of widgets or services are sold each month for a great Return on Investment (ROI). Slow-moving salespeople who make it through the recruiting process into a high-activity selling environment don't last long. It stresses them out. The pace is just too fast for them to maintain regular sales results above a minimum standard.

It's the same with horses. Some race, some pull wagons. You don't put a racehorse in front of a wagon. And you don't place a draft horse on a one-mile track. Their genetic makeup allows each to excel in different working environments. Physically, they are made for certain tasks and payloads delivered per hour.

By the way, we've got a couple of horses; pets that eat money, not grass. They appear to eat grass, but I assure you they eat money. One of them is easy to care for and handle. She's a real sweetheart. You can hug her and she will stand easily with minimal movement. But not Azam, an Arabian with a personality that's spirited and mischievous. He sprints around the field, removes boards from the fence, and tests his limits all the time. He's got to be moving. It's in his nature.

Do high-paced workload environments that require you to employ social skills with multiple personalities and people stress you out? Can you do this type of work month after month, year after year? Working this way is in the nature of a high-activity sales professional. If you're an entrepreneur without a quick-wired personality, in an industry with a fast sales cycle, through sheer will power you might be able to sell enough until you can hire a more suitable salesperson than yourself. Just realize that the do-it-now stress you will experience is fundamental to producing a healthy cash flow.

High-activity salespeople manage multiple selling tasks with an emphasis on doing activities. They race through the day and work in a flurry of activities and controlled emotions to achieve sales goals of three to five sales per day, week, or month depending upon the company they work for and its market. This means continuous prospecting activity and face-to-face selling situations.

I love to be around these high-flying salespeople: the Jessicas and Erics. Swirling with a vigorous and action-oriented nature, they work to make things happen in short bursts. Sending out emails, throwing presentations together, sprinting out the door, and closing sales. It's contagious and exciting—one big adrenaline rush—to be around the racehorses of many of our nation's sales teams.

The best ones keep the most important or critical sales activities at the right levels. They know that after every 30-31 day period the clock starts again for next month's sales and cash flow. Action is continuous and uninterrupted. Paperwork is pushed to a day's periphery. Prime time is used for prospecting and appointments.

Slowing down their new appointment rate is a high-activity salesperson's recipe for disaster. It's something that many entrepreneurs experience a few months in each year, especially if they have to install what they sell. If the prospecting and face-to-face appointments begin to slow, sales begin to trickle and cash flow drops.

So, what are the critical sales activities for a high-activity professional? What activities are of crucial importance? Which ones are essential for healthy cash flow?

CRITICAL SELLING ACTIVITIES

1. **Find new prospects.**
2. **Hold first appointments.**
3. **Conduct closing presentations (present quotes).**

The purpose of this book is to help you reach your sales goals and increase your income through better activity management of critical selling activities or *Right Levels of Right Activities*^{TM}. Those salespeople who manage their time to the right levels of right activities will achieve their income goals. This is the key factor for making the amount of money a rep desires from commissionable income. It is fundamental, and to borrow a football cliché, it's basic 'blocking and tackling.' Even so, there are only a few companies who truly manage the critical selling activities in a fast-moving sales process.

Find New Prospects. Not just any prospects, but targeted ones that meet your profile of an ideal customer or client. Set appointments with the most likely people or companies who fit your description of a best customer.

High-activity sales professionals do prospecting activities on most days of the week. This includes generating leads and then prospecting them for new appointments. When you watch successful high-activity salespeople at work, you find them sifting through people discovered through various lead generation methods. (We'll explore this definition further and how to find prospects in the section on lead generation.)

If you ever wondered why the term "prospecting" found its way into the sales vocabulary, you can understand from a description of those who explore for minerals. In the hills of Tennessee, my home state, I once watched an amateur miner sift for gold from the Little River in the Smoky Mountains. He reached into the water and sand with his pan and swirled the mixture around watching for flakes of gold to appear. As he explained the process and proudly displayed past nuggets he had found, I saw a fierce determination and optimism in his explanation and demonstration.

I've always found this same determination and optimism in great salespeople as they pan and sift through crowds of people at trade shows or cold-call on the phone. Even current customers get this same scrutiny for new products or services they may need.

Great salespeople spend a consistent block of time fighting to get in front of new prospects. They have to find and set appointments with the right number of prospects each month to reach their goals.

Hold first appointments. These are first time appointments with new prospects. During these appointments, possible new customers provide information about their needs, problems, and situation.

Do you know how many first appointments you hold each month? Do you know how many of them lead to closing presentations and quotes? If not, then how do you know if you're active enough to reach your goals? Even those who lead sales forces in performance can benefit from understanding their activity numbers. If they understood their numbers, how much further would they surge ahead and how high would their income grow? In my experience, it's a minimum of 30%.

Think about medical doctors. Even if they don't review their appointment levels, physicians must see enough new patients at an average cost per visit to achieve their income goals and pay their staff, insurance, etc. High-activity sales professionals experience the same math running through their activities to generate their results. Even if they don't understand the math, it still sits there as an underlying and critical component in their goal achievement.

You must hold a certain number of these first appointments each month to create enough closing opportunities to reach your goals. Medical doctors listen to needs and problems and propose solutions. High-activity sales professionals operate in the same manner (unless of course they are stimulus-response salespeople, which I will explain and talk about later).

Do closing presentations. These are the appointments in which you present a product or service solution, its profitable benefits for a prospect, and the investment, and then seek a yes or no from the customer or client. In many organizations, these are called quotes or deals in the pipeline or sales funnel. In the insurance field, it's their inventory of possible sales still in progress.

Interestingly, these moments of truth and decision occur for dentists, consultants, and those quoting HVAC systems. And, they happen on a regular basis for those professionals doing well. **When closing opportunities fall, sales plummet.** This decrease in quoting levels can be traced to a low number of first appointments. It can also be influenced by the quality of prospects, by how well they match up to the ideal customer profile. Compare this to the fact that if you ask enough people to marry you, you will eventually get a yes. But will this yes lead to a quality long-term relationship if the potential fiancé has objectionable but unconsidered personality and character qualities?

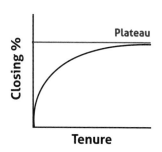

Of course, your closing ratio, the number of quotes you must make to get a sale, will also be impacted by face-to-face skills and techniques. However, since this percentage will plateau even for the best salespeople, activity management will have a dramatic impact on every sales rep's income from commissions.

New closing opportunities (often thought of as quotes) must be kept at a steady stream, the strength of which can be mathematically determined. This math is often unconsciously kept by the best salespeople. It is there, whether you are aware of it or not.

NON-CRITICAL ACTIVITIES

Emails, phone calls, paperwork, internal meetings, and other duties are important but not critical to the health of a sales professional and a company. Great reps and companies minimize the time traps that keep salespeople in the office.

Years ago, a major wireless carrier conducted a time usage study for their business-to-business reps to discover how many hours per week reps spent face-to-face in selling situations. What do you think they found? 25 hours, 15, 10? No. Eight (8) hours. Less than 2 hours per day. The main culprit was after-the-sale customer service: billing, usage, technical and other questions and problems.

Do not disregard excellent customer service. It increases referrals, amount of products and services used per customer, and it improves the passion of a work culture. And, since customers pay our salaries, kid's college educations, etc., let's give them the WOW service of the online retailer Zappos that Ken Blanchard writes about in his book *Raving Fans*. That said, the Critical Selling Activities (CSAs) must get done at the right monthly levels to have healthy cash flow for a salesperson or a business. Keep customer service and other duties off a salesperson's calendar as much as possible. Find ways to keep yourself or the reps that work for you prospecting and in front of potential customers.

Prospecting, setting and holding appointments, and doing closing presentations at right levels help you manage your monthly sales and keep them consistent and aligned with income needs.

Enough new or first appointments lead to enough quotes. Enough quotes lead to the right number of sales. The *Right Levels of the Right Activities*™ held with the right people lead to sales goal achievement.

Chapter 5

TURNING LIFESTYLE GOALS INTO ACTIVITY LEVELS

Plenty of people want a better lifestyle even if they do not know how to make it a reality. Most of the ads we see make promises and tell us stories to persuade us that our life will be better in some way if only we will buy this or that. Seth Godin in his book, *All Marketers are Liars*, explains how we buy stories and fantasy even when we choose commodities to purchase like tea or coffee. What else can explain a $5 cup of coffee at Starbucks?

I don't believe in karma. However, I do believe in cause and effect, that the sum of a person's actions, combined with intent, will have a great effect on their future and desired state of affairs in this lifetime. While nothing is guaranteed, we can certainly make decisions that will increase or decrease the odds in arriving where we want to end up. Those decisions, in the working arena of this book, will focus on action. Swinging a hammer at a nail will put up more walls an hour than purchasing the materials. **In short sales cycles, first appointments will lead to more quotes than talking to co-workers or working to build spreadsheets.**

Dale Carnegie, the author of *How to Win Friends and Influence People*, stated: "Inaction breeds doubt and fear. Action breeds confidence and courage. If you want to conquer fear, do not sit home and think about it. Go out and get busy." For us as salespeople, let's add, "Go out and get busy doing the right levels of the right activities."

> *In short sales cycles, first appointments will lead to more quotes than talking to co-workers or working to build spreadsheets.*

Salespeople do need to get busy spending the majority of their time doing the critical selling activities. But how many of these activities must they do to reach their goals? How can a future lifestyle be turned into sales activity targets?

This is a mystery for most. In our experience, **more than 95% of high-activity salespeople in companies do not know how to manage activities instead of results. It's the same for entrepreneurs. Consequently, they do not know how many prospects to find, how many appointments to set and hold, or how many quotes to get out each month to achieve their goals. And they do not have a simple way to track these activities and their targeted levels.**

So, how do most small businesses keep from failing? Unfortunately, they don't.

If you relate at all to Jessica, Eric, Maria, or Jackson, our salespeople described earlier, and you're ready for what it takes to make a change, the next section will help you figure out how active to be to achieve your lifestyle goals. Using simple math it will back you through the sales process from income needed to prospects found. It will take the mystery out of reaching sales goals and commissionable income. It will help you manage the activities that control your income.

INCOME GOALS TO SALES GOALS

Previously, you determined the income you desire. Let's say it's $7,200 per month in commissionable income.

Next, using your own knowledge or the help of your sales manager or the company owner, determine the monthly sales required to earn the $7,200. With some thought and help from your sales manager, even if you sell multiple products, you can come up with a conservative rule of thumb for this calculation. If you need help to see this, contact us at **salesmanage.com** or **salesactivities.com** and I or my staff will help you.

If you are paid per sales dollar or gross margin dollar, arrive at the total revenue sold per month that will pay you $7,200.

Example:

A salesperson is paid 15% of total revenue. That salesperson must have $7,200 ÷ .15 = $48,000 total in revenue sold per month.

TOTAL NUMBER OF SALES

Next, calculate the number of sales you will need to close per month. To do this, estimate the average or mean dollars per sale.

Example:

If the average sale is $12,000, a salesperson must close $48,000 ÷ $12,000 = 4 sales per month.

SALES TO QUOTES

To arrive at the number of quotes presented each month, make a conservative guess at your closing percentage, if you don't yet have an actual sales history from which to get it.

Example:

Closing Percentage = 33%. Salesperson must submit a minimum of 4 ÷ .33 = 12 quotes per month.

QUOTES TO APPOINTMENTS

By thinking about the quality of your prospects, you can estimate the percentage of first appointments held that will result in a quote request and presentation. If the prospects are very well qualified before a first appointment is held, then the percentage of first appointments leading to a quote will be high. In some industries, this percentage is near 100%.

Example:

Opportunity Percentage = 80%. Salesperson must hold a minimum of 12 ÷ .8 = 15 first appointments

APPOINTMENTS TO PROSPECTS

For the sake of discussion, let's estimate that a great salesperson will keep twice the number of prospects needed for a month's first appointments.

CRITICAL SALES ACTIVITIES

Therefore, to earn $7,200 in the example shown, *the magic ratio of critical selling activities is* 30 • 15 • 12 = 4 sales

30 prospects found

15 first appointments held

12 quotes presented

4 sales closed

And, then the month begins again with the same activity and more predictably, the same or better results.

THE ACTIVITY WIZARD NEVER SLEEPS

In high-activity selling, a direct mathematical relationship exists between activity levels and sales goals. In other words, there is a formula between critical selling activities and results. Doing the right amount of certain actions leads to specific results (sales and income).

It's as if there is an underlying activity wizard who never sleeps. His math is always the same and he hides away keeping count but never sharing his numbers with the salespeople he watches. They run on unaware of his presence. Yet, he's always there, always the same. His math is always present and working for or against their needs.

What they do not know is they can change the wizard's math. Here's how: Sales reps can qualify prospects better before setting an appointment to make sure more of them result in presentations. They can call to verify appointments so that more of the ones they set are held. They can change the ratios in the numbers by getting better in a variety of ways. In the previous example, if the rep's closing rate goes from 33% to 50%, then the ratio changes to 30 • 15 • 12 = 6. That's exciting—two more sales per month equals $3,600 per month or $43,200 more per year!

(A) Prospects to (B) First Appointments to (C) Presentations (quotes) = (D) sales = income achieved for lifestyle needs

For our example above, a rep is paid $7,200 in commissions for closing 4 sales. Those sales are a result of winning one third of the 12 quotes presented. Those 12 quotes occurred because of 15 first appointments and those appointments were set and held from a database of prospects with 30 or more names and numbers. And, where did the names come from? Lead generation activities!

Activity, activity, activity. Critical Selling Activities. The sacred use of available and premium selling TIME.

Remember, whether you understand or care about your numbers, the activity wizard is always there secretly counting and predicting your results, adding or taking from your lifestyle. Why not pay attention to his math and manage your activities according to the numbers? Why not do this and help yourself and your family? You can do this. Will you? Yes!

WORKING SMART LEADS TO LIFESTYLE CHANGES

What if someone didn't tell you what was par on every hole of a golf course and just sent you out to play a round? What if there were no yardage markers in the fairways? How would that affect your ability to score well? You would eventually get the ball in the hole and then find out your score. But, throughout the round, you wouldn't be able to manage your activities, select your clubs, or make adjustments to affect your results. With yardage markers and knowing how many strokes you need to make par, your chances increase for a better score. This is true for those with good or bad skills.

Picture a coach keeping track of your score on this course and beating you up for your results. Your golf coach keeps berating you to improve your scoring and shots per hole, but offers no guidance during the game. Salespeople experience this same situation when working for someone who pounds on them for results without coaching to a process. Entrepreneurs may do this to themselves as well because they just do not know what they do not know.

I want to help you change this. I want to help you work hard <u>and</u> smart. By managing your critical selling activities and their ratios, you will see improvements in sales and income. You will understand the cause and effect between sales and activity. You will not beat yourself up for results, but instead you will keep your head down and work on improving the quality and quantity of sales activities that make a difference. You will do the right levels of the right activities and while you do them you will learn to change things for the better. You will become a successful high-activity sales professional by turning your lifestyle goals into activity goals.

Chapter 6

INSPIRE YOURSELF!

A t this point on our journey together, through a trail of critical selling activities and their numbers, we find ourselves faced with a need to change our activity levels. This need to change, in the form of greater clarity and understanding, reveals a new direction for high-activity sales excellence. In the struggle to achieve, build, and provide for our fiscal needs, we find the journey better marked for our prosperity. A roadmap, partially drawn, lies in our hands.

Now, we must motivate ourselves. We must find a reason that will spur us on to greatness. Yes, greatness. As Jim Collins explains, in the first pages of *Good to Great*, very few churches, people, businesses, or other organizations strive to be great. Good, yes; great, no. And so, they are faced with continuing mediocrity and its negative effects.

As an example, consider the financial stewardship of the money we make. The growing debt in American financial statements and declining savings accounts point to mediocrity in this important area of our lives. Thus, we live out the negative effects of interest rates and monthly payments. Wouldn't it be simpler if we worked to be debt free and savings rich? So, why don't we? I think it's because even though we're motivated at times, we are not inspired.

▼ ▼ ▼

You now arrive again at a familiar point in life. You are faced with evidence that says, "Learn something new. Practice new skills. Change your habits." We've all been here before at the precipice of something new and better for us. It's a moment we will experience again and again in different quests to reach for things that are good for us.

We usually read more about motivation than inspiration. Somehow motives seem tangible while inspiration seems like divine guidance. We strive to learn how to motivate ourselves. We sincerely want to learn how to get ourselves to do what it takes to reach our goals, to fill out paperwork, to follow a sales process, to be better parents, to grow spiritually, etc. But in the doing we miss the inspiration that motivates.

From earliest recorded history to the present, teachers have addressed the subject of motivating people. In the twentieth century, theories like B.F. Skinner and Pavlov's dog swept our culture. Remember, ring a bell and the dog salivates if it has been conditioned to do so. The dogs did, and so will people.

While animals and people do make conditioned responses, people are at times unpredictable because of the human spirit residing deep within them. They make decisions based on that spirit. You can't control them. Just remember Victor Frankl's words from *Man's Search for Meaning*. "The one thing you can't take away from me is the way I choose to respond to what you do to me. The last of one's freedoms is to choose one's attitude in any given circumstance." Those are inspiring words from a prisoner in one of Germany's concentration camps in World War II.

Motivation often involves thinking about incentives, or it means striving to stimulate others into wanting to do something. It eventually turns into attempts at control: how to control another person, even oneself. This notion that we can control others is an illusion and leads to dictatorship, not motivation. Neither you nor they (even your kids) *have* to obey. Control is an illusion.

When you get a chance to see Anthony Hopkins (as anthropologist Ethan Powell) and Cuba Gooding in the movie *Instinct*, look for the scene where Ethan Powell, in prison for murder, teaches Cuba, the young psychiatrist Dr. Theo Caulder, that control is an illusion. When Ethan gets Dr.Caulder in a life-threatening position, it becomes apparent that the prisoner understands freedom better despite his jailed circumstances than the seemingly free psychiatrist who is actually in bondage to what others think of him. One is inspired from his heart by personal ideals and motives—the other motivated but by an outside world that controls him. By the end of the movie, the teacher becomes the student. The psychiatrist learns that control restricts inspiration and freedom. It does this by withholding or providing rewards as a means of personal measurement or to confirm a person's identity.

We need to understand inspiration for one very important reason only. It is to learn how to set up and maintain an environment in which we and those we lead can learn, grow, and thrive because of wise decisions. We want to discover an important cause or obligation that makes a lasting impression upon our hearts: one that moves us and those around us to important duties and goal achievement.

There's a nobler impact from inspiration as well. For a lasting effect, we need to inspire ourselves into greater efforts, greater enthusiasm, and greater creativity. To do this, we need to find purpose in what we do, a purpose in how we make things better for others, how our personal responsibilities contribute to improved lives, and how we help to achieve results that are important for the people we serve.

> *We want to discover an important cause or obligation that makes a lasting impression upon our hearts: one that moves us and those around us to important duties and goal achievement.*

As we open our eyes to the life we live, the adventure we are on, the battles we fight and who we strive to rescue, inspiration increases. We begin to also understand and fight for the valuable role we play in the health of a company or in our family. Then goals take on greater significance. And we are inspired.

For Steve, my business partner, working in the Alabama potato fields as a young child created a desire and motivation for a different future. When he stepped out of college, he stepped into a position with Northwestern Mutual at full commission and no salary. When those in leadership told him to do something, he did it. He made the calls and learned to manage his activity. He did not want to go back to the Alabama fields. Steve managed his activity and listened to advice from sales management for his own reasons not theirs. He motivated himself. He found inspiration by envisioning a better life for himself and his family.

Sometimes we all need help in finding inspiration in our lives. We motivate ourselves to do what others want done, to march in the direction they tell us. They ring a bell and we salivate. Our families, often broken and limited in parental direction, do not help us with purposeful adult maturity, especially if we've been allowed to float and we are not given potato fields of our own that inspire us with lasting motive.

Do you need motivation? Real motivation?

Where do you find the inspiration that creates lasting motivation? Where do you find reasons for sticking with something until you see it through? How do you mature to the point that you get up to fight a good fight every day for something that's important to your life?

I realize that many of you may not be inspired to work toward greatness. For now, you may just want to move away from survival and get some breathing room between yourself and failure. But consider that greatness, if it comes from inspiring motives, can't be compared to the achievements of others. In other words, greatness, if truly found in things that inspire, will have a different substance in one person than in another. What will set one person free will be merely a stepping-stone to someone else. Greatness then lies in progress away from the things that bind and block us. It's relative to the individual and to him or her alone.

What does greatness mean for Eric? Or Jessica? Isn't it obvious? Eric has to bring his wife home. He has to do it. What do you have to do? Jessica wants to leave, far behind, the quality of living she experienced with her mom even though her mom was a great mom, perhaps even an inspiring one, who pointed the way out.

As one of two children, Jessica watched her mom going to school at night and working by day as a secretary. She saw her mom cope with one child with a learning disability, a tight budget, back problems, and an ex-husband that didn't see his kids or pay his child support. But, there was always love at the door for her little daughter, who helped out with dishes, clothes, and by cleaning the homes of other people.

Later, Jessica learned to put work into an inspired new life with coaching and help from a caring manager. If her manager or coach said do 'this or that,' she did 'this or that.' She worked to get her activity levels high enough to build a new life for herself and she gave back to her mom in appreciation.

Remember my business partner, Steve, and his potato fields. Newly married and just out of college, Steve was only four years removed from backbreaking labor. Imagine a tractor pulling a plow, conveyor belt moving as potatoes were lifted and dropped to the ground. As a young man, Steve picked up the potatoes and put them in baskets placed in the field. He received 25 cents for each basket filled. Then, for $2.25 an hour, Steve carried the baskets to the truck and later from the truck to the washing barn.

That experience was motivating, yes. The money was important to a young man going to college. But inspiring? He found inspiration believing in a promising career that would provide a future very different from his past. The discipline required to reach it brought him and his family freedom from the potato fields.

Do YOU need motivation? Real motivation? I'm sure the answer is yes. It might be pressed down under years of following and taking orders, but it is there. Desire lies in the genes, waiting to be released. That's what I believe.

Get started and be inspired by forming a strong purpose for your work. Out of it will spring reasons for bringing accountability and new forms of discipline to your sales actions. Commit. Burn the boats of bondage. Take the new land, the new life, the better lifestyle. Work for it. Really work for it.

What is it about movies like *Lord of the Rings* or *Gladiator* that bring in billions of dollars? Purpose, standards, a cause. An adventure, battles, and a rescue, many rescues. People, who pay to see these movies, find life in the purposeful actions of the characters. And, I believe there's something else. It's tough and not easy. **We love to watch stories of perseverance where someone makes it through and beats the odds. We love to watch others overcome difficulties and win. That's because I believe we are born to take on challenges. Their tough moments help put meaning into our lives.**

We can make our lives meaningful with budget numbers to achieve, sales to close, children to put through school, and homes to make better. We fight against inflation, deflation, bad transmissions, and credit card debt. We fight to get in front of prospects, fill the needs of customers, and manage cash flow. Our world is one large movie set and we are its main characters with important parts to play.

Begin to build an environment in which you make a choice to be inspired. This motivation will naturally drive you to purposeful results. One way to do this is to get around what inspires you; for example books, movies, plays, and people. Look for inspiration and you will find it. If it is deep and lasting, it will drive you to do your best for the benefit of others, to strive for perfection and to achieve important goals. Now, go do this. You can.

Chapter 7

ACTION STEPS—GOALS AND DIRECTION

There really is a science behind activity management and what high-activity sales professionals do to achieve their goals. *A systematic study of a high-activity sales professional's use of time reveals an important fact. The lifestyle they can afford is directly connected to the levels of critical sales activities they do.* Even if they are not aware of his connection, the activity wizard keeps a firm control on their income and goal achievement.

Accepting the math behind the *Right Levels of Right Activities*™ helps to ensure sales goal achievement if we, as sales professionals, discipline ourselves to hit activity targets. If we operate at calculated activity levels, with calculations based on conservative assumptions, we increase the chances that we can meet or exceed our desired commissionable income. We can then look at improving other achievement variables like face-to-face skills and prospect qualification. The first improves the closing ratio of quotes to sales; the second improves the opportunity ratio of first appointments to quotes. (We'll talk more about this in Part II—Leads and Appointments).

As our professionalism, reputation and customer base strengthen, we can see our ratios change and our numbers continue to improve. That is, of course, if we do not reduce the number of critical sales activities done each month. With an increase in referrals, average sales size, or closing ratios, we can be less active and earn the same amount of money.

Even top performers can benefit and teach themselves to reach greater heights by understanding the connection between activity and results.

▼ ▼ ▼

Answer 6 questions to know the right activity levels for the income you need …

1. What is the **income** that will provide the lifestyle you want?

2. What **annual sales** will give you this income (in revenue or widgets)?

3. How many **sales** will you need to close to reach the annual sales goal? (Use a conservative guess of revenue or widgets per sale.)

Change this to a monthly sales goal by dividing by 12.

4. Based on a closing percentage, how many **quotes/month** will it take?

5. Based on an opportunity percentage, how many **first appointments/month** will it take to get out the quotes each month?

6. Knowing your first appointment level, how many prospects will you need to add each month?

(Note: You will need to estimate the following to answer the questions above: (1) appointments to quotes ratio, (2) quotes to sales ratio, and (3) average revenue or widgets per sale.

▼ ▼ ▼

I believe most of us do not want to do the least possible; we really want to grow up into adults with important things to accomplish in our lives.

So, inspire yourself with a desire to make life better than minimal production and limited options. Really want something. Find a reason for living that makes you act with maturity toward time and its use. Look around for role models and remember that inspiration is always connected to purpose and responsibility.

You find inspiration in a person, a story, or a past event, and your motivation is a direct result of its power on your beliefs. The movies and real life heroes and heroines that capture us in a good way strengthen our hearts for a noble cause. As we watch, we see them behave in the interest of others and sacrifice themselves and their time in a worthy manner. The best behave in authentic ways—not without flaws or weaknesses—but also with attitudes and beliefs that, in the end, strengthen their resolve to win. Watch, read about, and listen to these heroes and heroines. Notice the will of men and women who do admirable things.

I remember my sister-in-law, Sherry, who, worked hard to support two children. As a nurse with years of service she was faced with hospitals now requiring degrees for her position. Since she had a high school education, she began to go to school at night to earn her bachelor's degree. Twenty years later, at night, she earned a doctorate. And through it all, she supported her children, loved them, sacrificed for them, and provided for them. She also gave them the same will to grow that kept her going for all those years.

Move forward. Do what's important with your time. You can do the *Right Levels of the Right Activities.*™

Part II

TUNING UP YOUR ENGINE FOR LEADS AND APPOINTMENTS

Does thou love life, then do not squander time.
Make use of time, let not advantage slip.
WILLIAM SHAKESPEARE

Chapter 8

'TALKIN' AND 'FISHIN' AND 'LOOKIN' FOR GOLD

I loved my grandfathers, both of them. My mom's dad, Papaw, brought me up with a rod and reel in my hand. Early in the morning, at 5 a.m., he would awaken me for breakfast and we would board a bus going to Cherokee Dam in Jefferson City, Tennessee. Carrying peanut butter sandwiches and fishing gear, we would start at the dam and fish all day along the lake's bank until we arrived at the state campgrounds. As we walked, there wasn't much "talkin," just "fishin."

As a youngster, I copied whatever Papaw did—the distance he threw his bobber, line, hook, and worm from shore and the number of times he turned his reel as he moved the bobber in jerks and stops across the water, jiggling the bait in a way that was enticing to the fish. And, boy did we catch fish, a whole croker sack full of them. One time as we turned a point of land pushing out into the lake and started around on the other side and into another cove, my grandfather remarked, **"Those who catch the most fish keep their bait in the water more than others do."** What he meant was that fooling around with time, skipping rocks, watching the birds, were all great things to do. But, when it's fishing time you'd better be fishing or the other guy will beat you (he believed in competitive fishin'). If you don't keep your bait in the water you won't have enough fish to feed everyone back home.

Keep your line in the water and you'll catch more fish, perhaps enough to feed your family. Work to provide good food for those you love , not survival level fast food meals, but very good nourishing fare.

Find enough leads and prospect them. Nothing is as certain as the production that follows when you fish in the right waters.

▼ ▼ ▼

It's difficult to find a dictionary that refers to a lead as something a salesperson finds important. But it's a common term in the sales world. And, if handled well, leads create a healthy foundation for the performance of high-activity sales professionals.

> **Definition: "lead"—someone that is quite possibly a prospect, quite possibly a person interested in the product(s) or service(s) you sell.**

That brings up the term "prospect." How is a prospect different from a lead? **A prospect is simply a lead that you decide to do a**

sales activity with; it's someone who, based on the evidence at hand, could fit an ideal customer profile. In other words, if you get a stack of leads from some source, a few of these leads might have more potential than others. And, when you choose some to call and qualify further, and perhaps set a first appointment with, they become prospects at the top of your sales funnel. Then you are prospecting, "looking for gold in them thar hills" as the old timers say.

Great salespeople learn to visually manage sales goal achievement as if working down and through a funnel. At the top, leads pour in from a lead generation machine that is operated by either the salesperson or the company or both.

The salesperson chooses which leads to take down into the funnel. The first stage occurs when the salesperson attempts to set appointments. After further work, a few prospects go to the second stage—the First Appointment. Fewer still go to the third stage— Sales-In-Progress, those prospects with quotes not yet decided upon. The Sales-in-Progress that close become SALES $$$ out the bottom!

Lead generation is at the top; sales are at the bottom. If you keep your first appointments and quote production steady, then you actually earn a certain number of dollars per hour of lead generation. This may be $500 per hour, $1000, etc. You also earn dollars per hour of prospecting as you work (dialing and calling) to set appointments with promising leads! Think of lead generation and prospecting in dollars earned per hour as these tasks are helping you achieve your income goals each month.

In sales, you achieve income goals from each hour of prospecting! Why? Because, whatever closing rate you achieve, continuous prospecting at a right level keeps your income production close to your needs.

THE ENGINE

What is a lead generation engine? It's a number of different activity channels that stream the names of potential prospects in your direction. Think of it as an engine with different "lead" inputs with each contributing leads that you can qualify as targeted prospects. The steady flow from these "lead channels" fuels the engine that keeps you relevant as a salesperson. Without it, sales slow to a trickle or stop altogether. With it, you form a foundation for monthly income without great peaks and valleys. It also provides the pressure within your sales funnel that propels you to a higher income.

A rocket achieves momentum from an initial burst of power and then keeps its trajectory on an upward path until its engines begin to lose fuel. We all know what the path looks like next and it isn't a soft landing. Many salespeople live through ugly cash flow swings and an up and down trajectory. To minimize income swings, the best salespeople keep the pressure up on lead generation and prospecting activity. Much misery or happiness can be traced back through the swings to an insufficient or sufficient power source behind lead generation.

DESCRIBE YOUR LEAD GENERATION MACHINE

When we ask small company owners, sales managers, or salespeople to put together a lead generation engine, they often look puzzled and do not readily respond. However, they immediately know the importance of the focus.

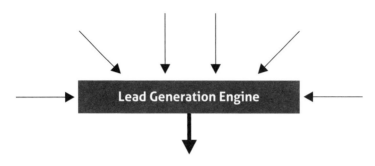

Many people responsible for sales performance do not think about lead generation as a machine with inputs that eventually produce an adequate number of leads to prospect. Very few seem to look at lead generation as a designed system (or engine) or intentionally construct its parts for maximum flow.

Small businesses do spend money for advertising, trade shows, and other forms of lead generation. It's just not done as a designed machine with inputs targeted at certain markets, customer profiles, and types of businesses.

Think of lead generation as a machine. What activity sources fuel its inputs? What is your marketing calendar for the next quarter? Which sources produce best with the least cost per lead? How many leads do you need each sales period? How will you track lead disposition (who receives them) and subsequent actions and results?

RESPONSIBILITY FOR LEAD GENERATION

There are actually two engines for a sales team's lead generation machine. One belongs to the company and the other belongs to each salesperson on the team.

Some companies accept most of the responsibility for lead generation and supply all the leads that its salespeople prospect. Other companies expect salespeople to continually supply their own leads. Others share lead generation with their salespeople.

Which of the examples above describe your company? How well do you understand what your company will do and what you will do to generate leads? How are those responsibilities divided?

LEAD SOURCES AND CHANNELS

There are many types of lead sources to choose from. The ones you choose will depend on the profile of an ideal customer. In the next section, you will define an ideal customer. You will then look for the best ways to obtain leads (names of people or companies) who fit that definition. Next, you will decide how to approach and set appointments with typical decision makers most likely to have a set of needs and problems your company can fill or solve with its products or services.

Typical types of lead sources for high-activity sales professionals include: customers and their referrals, advertising, trade shows, networking through centers of influence, vendors, lead exchange groups, chamber of commerce events purchased lists, public lists, trade journals, driving around, target market conferences, driving or walking around target areas, existing customers, clubs, your web site, other web sites, speeches, and articles you distribute. Each source provides a certain number of leads; some provide more than others. *Lead quality per channel varies, so stop doing what doesn't work well or produce enough leads for time invested and focus on what does.*

DIAGRAM IT TO SEE IT

Develop a lead generation engine to give you enough of the right leads which you can then prospect through first appointments. To do that well, answer the following questions. How many prospects do you need to find each month to meet first appointment goals? Where will you go to find leads to those prospects? From what channels?

Do you currently depend on one or two channel activities for your lead sources? Multiple lead sources, more than three, provide a greater chance of sales goal achievement.

Diagram how you will generate leads for yourself. When you draw your lead generation plan and its various channels, ask yourself, "Why do I choose each lead source? Why do I believe each will produce qualified leads?"

Also remember, your best source of leads for new business often comes from past or current customers. These rank first in lead strength followed by any referrals they provide.

Centers of influence (COIs) refer high quality leads as well. COIs are people who like you and your services and products and will use their influence to help you get in front of potential new prospects. Great COIs often have their ear to the ground in parts of the marketplace where they hear about problems and needs serviced by your product or service. We may refer to them as "movers and shakers," but not necessarily. A productive center of influence can be a well-placed engineer, manager, or worker. Oftentimes, a great COI is an existing customer. If you find some good COIs, they can help you be the first to knock when the need is present for a prospective customer.

Now, draw your Lead Generation Engine with its activity channels as a planning step. Then, work them to produce enough leads for qualified prospects. Always be open to replacing or adding lead generation channels. Bottom line—design and operate a lead generation engine to produce a certain number of qualified prospects each month to meet your first appointment goals.

BACK TO JESSICA'S STORY

Jessica began with great desire and drive to succeed. At the beginning of her employment, she was swept up into a coaching process that helped manage her activity levels. After setting an income goal, her sales manager, Barbara, coached her into important lead generation activities.

Barbara directed Jessica to investigate and join a BNI (Business Networking International) group. In that group, she learned how to network with other sales professionals, share leads, and reach prospective customers through other relationships.

Barbara also taught Jessica to send approach letters to decision makers at target companies. And, Jessica learned how to follow a systemized approach to setting appointments by phone. Later, she learned how to cold call without an approach letter being sent. As she missed or completed a sale, Barbara taught her young superstar how to ask for referrals.

Jessica also attended chamber of commerce meetings and important trade show events. She used the networking skills learned at BNI and from her sales manager to introduce herself, obtain cards, and follow up with calls for appointments.

Jessica became a self-promoting professional and generated her own leads to supplement those provided by the sales manager. In many cases, her leads were better than those she received from the company.

Jessica scheduled lead generation activities as she began in her sales position. This contributed to her great start. She learned to place important events, call-

NOVEMBER
17

ing hours, and other lead generation activities on a calendar and worked to keep those times sacrosanct, protected from distraction and change. Why Barbara coached Jessica into this routine can be traced to a water hose. Yes, a water hose!

WATER HOSES AND LEAD GENERATION

We have a hose in the barn to keep the horses' tubs full of crystal clear drinking water. Each horse needs about 10-12 gallons of water a day up to 20-25 gallons on hot, humid days. We keep the tubs filled so they can drink freely at anytime in cold and warm weather.

Think about lead generation as a hose that you keep turned on at all times. It services the top of your sales funnel with an ever-present flow of prospects, new customers, and income flow. Think about being on the receiving end of this income that is dedicated to providing for basic and lifestyle needs. You need consistent lead generation. It must not be turned off while you are a high-activity sales professional. Its continuous flow keeps you living well at the lifestyle you have chosen. It is the basis of your work and living.

Keep it on and keep the pressure steady. Always.

Chapter 9

FINE TUNING TOWARD TARGETED PROSPECTS

While many of you may not have fishing experience, I know you can still understand that some waters do not contain enough fish or the right kind of fish. For a young person, it takes the wisdom of a grandfather to teach you where to fish.

It's the same for high-activity sales professionals. A good sales manager or mentor can teach you which "waters" to work in for maximum efficiency and effectiveness, waters that contain the right levels of the right leads to prospect.

Obviously, a lead generation engine will produce lots of opportunities—many of them dead ends or not within your target market. Its channel inputs, seminars, trade shows, cold calling, etc., produce a worthwhile quantity and quality of leads.

As a high-activity sales professional, you realize the importance of spending enough time with the right people each commission period. *Right Levels of Right Activities,*™ with the right people, leads to happiness as a sales professional. It leads to qualified first appointments with those who have a need for your product or service.

This makes prospecting time more productive and results in higher numbers achieved from a specified number of first appointments and quotes.

FINE TUNING YOUR ENGINE

Make your lead generation engine an efficient tool for yourself. Work to find leads and set appointments with those people or businesses that meet your characteristics of an ideal prospect. To do this well, decide what the ideal prospect profile looks like. First, write down the needs and problems that people face that you fill and solve. Then, consider geography, income levels, target industry, decision maker level and titles, employee count, size, income, sales, etc., and other possible modifiers. Now, choose the best possible characteristics of an ideal customer profile with any appropriate numbers and measurements that you might include.

Think carefully about what you choose as characteristics. You may want to choose those types of customers who provide the most profit for the least amount of time necessary in the sales cycle. Perhaps, product or service delivery can be more efficiently delivered to one type of customer versus another type. Think about the kinds of characteristics important for you.

Possible considerations include:

- Geographical location: local/out-of-state, area of town, international, etc.
- Vertical markets: churches, boating, manufacturing (types of), dentists
- Infrastructure: multi-site, technology familiarity, etc.
- Employees: number of, type
- Size of company
- The individual or person
- Needs and problems to fill and solve

GEOGRAPHICAL LOCATION

Where do you go to pursue customers or clients? Does it make sense to generate leads from a specific area? Will this help you use time better and increase your prospecting efficiency and first appointment levels?

Perhaps you can network more effectively if you stay in one area. What about travel costs? The cost per sale? Delivery costs and the time necessary to service multiple clients in different locations?

I've seen salespeople ignore all the business within a two mile radius of their home. If the people or businesses around your home fit the profile of an ideal customer, find ways to generate leads there. Work to 'own' the area around where you live.

VERTICAL MARKETS

What vertical markets make more sense to pursue leads in than others? Does your service or product provide benefits that certain markets find more valuable than others?

If you focus on one to three vertical markets, will that help you understand customer needs, their lingo, and business situations? Will you therefore appear more familiar with their challenges and problems and more able to expertly design customized solutions?

Several years ago, I focused exclusively on credit unions. In doing so, I became very familiar with their purpose, struggles, and language. For example, they did not refer to those they served as customers. They referred to them as members. My understanding of this one important point of uniqueness (and others) helped them see me as a professional who understood them. My referrals rose and I soon found myself in Canada pursuing and earning business from the credit unions there. Unlike banks, they were one big fraternal type of community and they share important vendors among themselves.

INFRASTRUCTURE

What brick and mortar requirements fit what you need to find in your best customers? Think about this and answer the following questions. As you reply to each, how do your responses impact where you look for leads?

- Do you want to handle multiple sites?
- Do you need a customer with certain technology capabilities?

- Do you work with companies with certain departments?
- Do you work with companies that have certain physical characteristics?
- Do you need to understand how a company communicates with itself and others?
- Are its training processes important to you?
- Do you need a customer to own a certain amount or type of equipment?
- Do you need to approach buildings of a certain type and structure?

OF EMPLOYEES OR TYPE OF EMPLOYEES

Will you only sell to target companies with a certain number of employees? Does the number of employees indicate something about their likelihood to buy what you sell?

Are there certain types of employees that need what you sell, for example, nurses, delivery personnel, or a particular type or all types of salespeople? Some products or services serve all kinds of employees and companies. Others serve only a very narrow niche like uniforms for policemen or basketballs for the NBA.

SIZE OF THE COMPANY

Is the size of a company's yearly revenue important? Should it be greater than one million dollars, one billion, or at some other production level? Does being a member of the Inc 500 or Fortune 500 reveal something you want in an ideal customer? Perhaps the company needs to be fast-growing, or maybe a start-up, or privately held.

For example, the ideal customer profile for a wireless business-to-business rep could be any company with 100 employees and 25 existing handsets located within a 25 mile radius of town. An insurance representative might focus on individuals with a net worth of $1 million or more, living in an area with exclusive homes, valued at $500,000+ and who work as family physicians. A residential security professional may choose to look for signs of competitors or for neighborhoods with home values above $150,000 in the south part of town and with an above average number of reported break-ins.

By profiling ideal customers and targeting them, your lead generation engine becomes "fine-tuned" toward channels more likely to produce the perfect customer for you. You accomplish this tuning by choosing more appropriate places from which to generate leads. When you do this, you choose to spend prospecting time with higher quality leads.

This fine-tuning also helps those who want to help you. When you introduce yourself to a networking group or explain your customer profile to a center of influence (COI), you make them more effective at finding new leads for you. Your clear understanding and communication makes it clear how others can help you find quality prospects. This makes subsequent referrals and COI networking increase in value.

THE PERSON OR INDIVIDUAL

For those of you that sell to the individual man or woman at home or work, please think about a person's characteristics that make them a good prospect for your product or service. Your description of an ideal prospect profile might include any of the following: income level, size and value of home, type of employment, or dress requirements at work. Do they reside in subdivisions, gated communities, and resort areas or in rural communities? Does whom they associate with make a difference? What typical need or problems do they have that require your products and services?

AN IMPORTANT EXERCISE

Look back over the preceding sections for inspiration and direction, and then write down how you would describe an ideal prospect. To continue to strengthen your description, write down answers to the following question as if a COI asked it, "How would I recognize a great lead for you?" Be able to answer this in one minute or less. This exercise will help you better define for yourself appropriate channels for lead generation. It will also help you better inform others in their efforts to refer better leads to you. Networking groups you belong to and centers of influence need this level of specificity from you. And you need it too.

ACTIVITY RATIOS IMPROVED

The fine-tuning of your lead generation engine improves activity ratios leading to your income and sales goal achievement. This happens because the people you target meet the profile for ideal characteristics that define those people more predisposed toward interest in your product or service. Therefore, the probability increases that they have a need or problem for which you can provide a solution.

When prospecting the right leads and making calls on the right people and companies, the percentage of first appointments from calls will grow because the probability of prospect interest is higher. In addition, the percentage of first appointments continuing forward in the sales process to a quote or presentation grows for the same reason.

Before you design your "Lead Generation Machine," decide the best prospect profile for your product. This profile contains the characteristics of customers for whom you most want to provide products and services.

When you begin to generate leads and then prospect them for first appointments, you will use an irreplaceable commodity—time. Use it well! Fish for leads within those businesses and from those people who have a greater probability of having the right characteristics of a potential customer. Stay away from those areas with a low density of target profile prospects.

SERIOUS FISHERMEN

When I'm serious about fishing, I focus on those areas with the greatest concentrations of the kind of fish I want to catch. If it's catfish, then I fish off the bottom of the lake. For bluegill, I fish along the shoreline and in shallow coves. If I want to catch trout, then I know the cold water of certain mountain streams will produce more trout than the placid waters of warm lakes.

Fast sales cycles usually involve a small amount of money and a quick decision as compared to longer sales cycles. To understand the money and criteria for purchasing doesn't require someone to stop and do strategic thinking. Lead generation methods are relatively simple. As the size of the sale grows, lead definitions may remain simple, but the rest of the sales process can stretch out beyond the 90-day window for high-activity sales professionals and each step in the sale requires thoughtful planning.

As high-activity sales professionals, we keep it simple. We work to find high-quality leads, and we narrow our lead generation activities to those providing the greatest quality and quantity of return. That's because we realize that the majority of our time must be focused on getting in front of people or fighting to get in front of them. We want to be just smart enough and strategic enough to get in front enough of the right people.

Chapter 10

PROSPECTING FOR GOLDEN APPOINTMENTS

Have you ever panned for gold, as I described earlier? Even today, there are people who know how to make a living wading in mountain streams and sifting all the lighter materials out of a pan leaving the heavier gold behind. Back and forth, left and right, the prospector sifts gold at places that meet his criteria for having gold deposits in the sediment.

A few years ago, we were fishing on the Little River in Townsend, TN when I saw a man panning for gold. He told me stories of nuggets found along the shore of the river and of gold mines upstream long ago. What was most interesting was watching him patiently searching among lots of sand and sediment for a precious mineral. Oh yes, he did reach into a sack and pull out some vials of gold he had found on previous prospecting trips.

Prospecting for gold and fishing are very similar to prospecting in sales. Both require looking in the right places and sifting through some rocks to find things that pay off or make the trip worthwhile. You can do any of these activities well if you have the right levels of the right activities, and in sales, with the right people.

Now it's time to prospect the leads you have and set first appointments with them. You want to set first appointments at the critical rate per month that you've calculated is necessary to meet activity management targets leading to your monthly sales and income goals.

Remember, first appointments lead to quotes, quotes lead to sales. The right amount of each with the right people (prospects) leads to sales goal achievement.

IMPORTANT: Before beginning any sales period—day, week or month—*start that period with a Prospects-in-Progress list.* This is a list of highest priority leads that you will work to set your target number of first appointments. You might also refer to this as your calling list for first appointments. The number of prospects on this list may need to be twice as great as the number of first appointments you must set each month.

SEVEN APPOINTMENT SETTING ABSOLUTES

1. **Schedule and protect phoning time.** Make this time sacrosanct and not easily replaced by another activity. Revere the time. Keep it untouchable. Block out the time on your calendar. Schedule everything else around it. It will take you "X" number of phone hours to set your critical number of first appointments.

2. **Call from 9:00 a.m. to 10:00 a.m.: Monday, Tuesday, Wednesday, and Thursday.** These are premium times for calling. Do not call for less than one hour. If necessary, call on Friday in order to secure your target number of first appointments set for the week.

3. **Be prepared to call with 15 phone numbers.** It may take 30 minutes to an hour to prepare for your calling hour. This is important because preparation will make your calling time more efficient and focused only on making calls and setting appointments.

4. **Average 15 dials per hour.** Average 2 appointments per hour. Decide to target X appointments set each day of calling. In other words, know what calling results you want for an hour or a day. Be specific with yourself.

5. **Work referred leads where possible.** "Mr. Jones, I'm a good friend of ..." The number of appointments set from referred leads is much higher than most leads you work.

6. **Work vertical markets as much as possible and where possible.** When you work a vertical market, this makes you more

effective in the sales process. Participating in several discussions makes you handle conversations in a more competent manner to the ears of the prospect, as your questions and advice are more homogeneous to their cultural terms.

7. **Script out responses to typically asked questions, fears, or concerns, but do not try to convince people.** Look for low hanging fruit (as Bill Good mentions in his book, *Prospecting Your Way to Sales Success*)—those willing to schedule an appointment. Leave other callers intact for future conversations and prospecting calls.

Scripting Characteristics

Yes, use a script. A good script will give you confidence and help you appear disciplined and prepared because, of course, you will be. To develop your own script, here are seven scripting rules to follow.

1. Get the right person on the phone.
2. Introduce yourself and explain how you received their name.
3. Ask permission to tell why you are calling.
4. Tell them what you do and why you are calling (strong benefit statement).
5. Seek permission to ask a few questions to see if there is a reason to schedule a visit.
6. Ask the questions.
7. Summarize their responses and ask for the appointment (Ask for the appointment at any time during the call if someone is obviously eager to meet.).

Scripting Examples

The next two examples represent a couple of scripts. One is for wireless business-to-business sales. The other is for a financial services firm installing an employee benefits program.

(Wireless)

1. Get the right person on the phone

"Who makes decisions in your company about wireless?"
"Will you please connect me with him (her)?"

2. Ask permission to tell them why you're calling.

"Mr. Jones? Good Morning, Mr. Jones. How are you today? GREAT! This is _____. I am the XYZ rep for this area. Do you have a minute to let me tell you why I'm calling?"

(Most say yes. If no, then ask them, "When would be the best time to call you back?")

3. Tell them why you're calling

"Mr. Jones, my job is to help companies either save on their rate plans or improve their service. Do you have a minute for me to ask 3-4 questions to see if there is a reason for us to talk further?"

(If not, then ask them, *"When would be the best time to call you back?"*)

4. If yes, ask ...

"Whom do you currently use as a carrier?"
"Who has been assigned to you as a rep?
"When did (she/he) someone last look at your rate plans, or do a rate plan analysis?"
"What do you need help with or what would you like to improve?"

5. *"GREAT, I believe there's a good reason for us to talk further (summarize this). May I meet with you this Wednesday or Thursday at 1:00 p.m.?"*

(Financial Services)

1. Get the right person on the phone

"Who makes decisions in your company about employee benefits programs?"
"Will you please connect me with him (her)?"

2. Ask permission to tell them why you're calling

"Mr. Jones? Good Morning, Mr. Jones. How are you today? GREAT! This is _____. I am the XYZ rep for this area. Do you have a minute to let me tell you why I'm calling?"

(Most say yes. If no, then ask them, "When would be the best time to call you back?")

3. Tell them why you're calling

"We help companies like yours accumulate and protect the wealth of their employees with a state-of-the art employee benefit program. Do you have a minute for me to ask 3-4 questions to see if there is a reason for us to talk further?"

(If not, then ask them, "When would be the best time to call you back?")

4. If yes, ask:

"How many employees do you have? How do you see this number changing?"
"How much do your employees understand about retirement options?"
"What type of employee benefits plan do you currently have?"
"What do you like about it and what would you like to change?"

5. *"GREAT, I believe there's a good reason for us to talk further. May I meet with you this Wednesday or Thursday at 1:00 p.m.?"*

In general, scripts are frameworks for a more balanced and targeted approach to appointment setting. However, it should not sound scripted. And, you are allowed to vary if the other person doesn't want to play along. It's been my experience that a script, in the long run, makes you a more effective person on the phone, especially if a well thought out introduction and set of questions have been developed in advance.

ACTIVITY MANAGEMENT PRINCIPLES

Were you surprised to learn earlier in this section that there really are people today who make a living panning for gold? They can even make $4000-5000 a month. But they know the best places to work and they are professional—prospectors who have learned to prospect in the most likely places. And, they realize just as high-activity sales professionals do, that consistent prospecting leads to consistent results and food on the table.

Make appointment setting a scheduled and protected habit. Keep phoning time at a consistent level even as you get busy! This smoothes out the peaks and valleys of sales production and helps steady cash flow by maintaining funnel pressure through each stage of the sales process and its critical selling activities: prospecting, setting and holding appointments, and presenting quotes.

Chapter 11

GOING ON FIRST DATES

First dates. Awkward? At times. And, then for me there was that 5'4" Italian that just melted my heart. It was perfect the first time out, just right. So it can happen.

I remember in college, running out of physical chemistry class one winter day right into my future bride (39 years in love today and still counting). I very boldly said, "Hi!" She just kept tooling right on down the hallway. I continued this for the next two classes until she stopped, looked up and me, and said, "What's your name? Do I know you?"

"Lance," I quickly got out. "Nope!" She replied, and off down the hall she went.

I followed her across campus, found out all I could about her, and the next time I saw her in the hallway right after class, I asked her out. That first date (appointment) was wonderful and we've been dating ever since.

▼ ▼ ▼

It's not always romantic or easy to find leads and then prospect them for first appointments. It's difficult. For many, it's the most troublesome part of the sales process. Why? Because of the energy it takes to initiate a meeting with a stranger and navigate the beginning moments with another complex human being. When you do meet, it's with someone who doesn't trust you or know if you're dependable or competent. They lift up interpersonal barriers of protection and defend themselves from your advances.

To make matters worse, many people do not think highly of the selling profession. Ask a group of people, "What's the first thing you think of when you hear the word salesperson?" More than 90 percent of the answers you hear will be negative: labels like Slick Willy, loud dresser, and dishonest.

And yet, we are compelled to develop people into customers who are accustomed to only buying from us. It's our job. Our profession requires us to obtain new customers to sustain our earnings. In the end, when we persevere, we enjoy clients who provide us with reoccurring revenue and great working relationships. At the beginning of the sales process, these new revenue sources start with the first date—a first appointment.

FIRST APPOINTMENTS—WHAT ARE THEY?

An *effective* first appointment is *one in which your skills reveal a person's need(s), want(s), or problem(s).* As the appointment progresses, a prospect may experience discomfort when discussing not having a need filled, a want satisfied, or a problem solved. This discomfort occurs as a result of words they say when answering your questions about their situation. You listen, paraphrase your understanding, ask other important and clarifying questions, nod at appropriate times and listen.

High-activity salespeople work toward making first appointments effective. To do this, they strive to understand the prospect's situation well enough to make a subsequent presentation a valuable use of time for everyone involved, including themselves. Salespeople who do not understand the importance of questions make themselves less effective in multiple ways. They:

- Dominate the conversation and fail to establish trust and rapport.
- Spend time with the wrong people: people they cannot help.
- Talk about the wrong things.
- Stress features and benefits of no interest to the prospect.
- Put together solutions that do not fill needs, satisfy wants, or solve problems.
- Do proposals or quotes with no chance of closing the deal.

As a result, they see lower rates of referral and repeat sales and create a negative effect on their sales productivity.

THE OBJECTIVE

High-activity salespeople pursue an objective in every first appointment. They desire to lead a discovery process in which both they and their prospects see a reason to put together and evaluate a proposal. The promise is simple. "Based on our appointment, and what has been discussed, I believe there is a reason for you to see a presentation (quote or proposal). Or, "I believe we can help you and I want to show you how." Or, "Thanks for your time, but at this time I don't think the timing is right for you (or for us)."

The span of time from appointment to close can be as little as 5 minutes in the sale of a wireless accessory or 90 days or longer for a complicated financial services agreement or commercial security installation. And of course, as the dialogues above allow, their answers to a rep's questions may lead to a decision not to present. They disqualify themselves.

So, a first appointment's objective is for both the salesperson and the prospect to see a reason for spending time further evaluating the salesperson's product or service. This presentation and quote may occur in a first appointment or in a subsequent appointment.

ACTIVITY MANAGEMENT

Please remember this for activity management by the numbers. **Minimally, to *count* as a first appointment, the prospect answers questions about an area related to the salesperson's product or service benefits.** If this occurs, a first appointment is counted even if the answers do not lead to a presentation or quote.

You may ask why I stress this counting rule. It's simple. If you begin to count first appointments as any meeting with a prospect, then the number of first appointments required to generate a quote increases. You may be led astray thinking your activity is at the right level with the right activities, when, in reality, your appointment to quote rate, the opportunity ratio, is too high. While you are "active," and perhaps working hard, you may in fact be kidding yourself by thinking your selling activity is great enough for your income achievement.

> Minimally, to count as a first appointment, the prospect answers questions about an area related to the salesperson's product or service benefits.

Meet with the right prospects at the right levels of right activities. To minimize appointments not leading to a quote, be sure to pay attention to the ideal prospect profile. Set appointments with the type of individuals, people, or businesses whose situation gives you a greater chance of providing a presentation and quote. Also, work to make sure that people understand the purpose of your call, which is to ask some pre-prepared questions about their situation and its needs and problems.

If you are a high-activity salesperson just meeting with prospects without doing an interview around their situation, you may not get enough quotes out to qualified prospects to feed yourself each month. I remember working with one salesperson whose first appointments levels were within his calculated requirements, but he did not produce enough quotes or close enough sales each month. When analyzing this activity, his sales manager and I discovered that seldom did he get someone to answer business development questions. Instead, he just socialized with them. The result? Not many of his first appointments led to quotes. Without enough quotes, there was not a way to hit the revenue numbers required of him. Consequently, the rep was always stressed in meeting budget.

He solved his dilemma by changing his definition of a first appointment. He began to pay attention to the quality of his leads. Most importantly, he began to ask prospects for permission to ask a few questions to see if there might be a reason to talk further about customized solutions for his company. When this happened, his quote production and sales increased.

AN IMPORTANT SKILL FOR HIGH-ACTIVITY PROFESSIONALS

LISTENING is *the number one face-to-face skill* used by high-activity sales professionals during first appointments. The best salespeople also magnify this skill by paraphrasing, taking notes, and summarizing a prospect's situation.

Asking business development questions is THE underlying skill supporting a salesperson's listening abilities. A SET of carefully designed need-development questions, starting with who, what, where, why, when, how, describe or tell, is *the best tool* used in a first appointment. Sales professionals design customized questions. They design them to get a prospect talking about the typical needs, wants, or problems people experience that cause them to buy a particular service or product.

A prospect's needs, wants, or problems vary from industry to industry. Examples include a family's personal safety or financial security, better connectivity and communication between family members, personal health and well being for a senior citizen, business productivity, etc. Make a list of these for your industry. Answer these two questions:

"What are the facts and information you must gather before recommending a product or service?"

"What are the needs or problems that typical customers have that influence their decision to buy what you sell?"

Then, start designing your need-development questions that cause them to talk about their needs, wants or problems. Here are some examples of great questions in three different industries. These were developed by sales leaders and salespeople I trained in that particular industry.

EMPLOYEE RETIREMENT PLANS

1. Tell me about your company and some information about its history.
2. What are/were your main goals for establishing a retirement plan?
3. How much is currently invested in your plan?
4. How many employees do you have? How do you see this number changing?
5. How much do your employees understand about retirement options?
6. What do you like about your current plan? What would you like to change?

7. What has caused you to look for an alternative investment source?

8. What has been most disappointing in your past experience with retirement plans?

9. Tell me about the company's cash flow and any funding limitations.

10. What opportunities and threats do you see for your business in the next five (5) years?

11. Describe what types of investment choices you would like to see. Tell me what you would like to see in your new plan.

12. What are your goals for retirement?

13. What criteria will you base your decision on? By when do you expect to decide?

14. Who, besides yourself, will be involved in a decision?

COMMERCIAL REAL ESTATE

1. Tell me about your business and your customers/clients.

2. Why do you want to dispose of your property? Why does it no longer work for you? Why are you moving?

3. What's important about its history?

4. Where do you plan to go (move)?

5. What is most important to you in the disposition of this property? How often do you want me to communicate progress? (Do this with some minimum frequency)

6. Tell me what you expect financially? How do you want this structured?

7. What does your timeline look like? When do you need the building sold?

8. What is the square footage of the facility?

9. Tell me your thoughts about the best uses of this building. What do you like best about it?

10. What environmental aspects have been investigated?

11. How close are you to cash flow crisis (with financing)? Using these rough numbers _____, how does that affect your ability to deal?

12. Who will I be working for directly: you, a team, or someone else?

13. Who, besides yourself, will be involved in the buying decision?

14. What relationships do you have with other realtor providers?

WIRELESS OR MOBILE PHONE DEVICES

1. Describe for me a typical day/week for you and your phone.

2. Tell me about your family. Ages of children? Extended family contact? How many people are in your household?

3. What type of phone do you use?

4. What do you (did you) like/dislike about your current (previous) phone?

5. What do you want to do with a phone other than make and take calls?

6. What phones have you looked at so far? Which ones did you like? Why?

7. What is your ideal or perfect phone? What would it do?

8. How often are you on the internet? Use a laptop? What about when you travel?

9. How often do you check your email? How important is to-the-minute delivery?

10. How much are you paying for your landline phone per month?

11. Describe your internet service at home. How often do you access the internet there?

12. Where do you work? What do you do? Number of employees? Laptops? Use of wireless?

13. Who was the personal rep assigned to you at _____? When was the last time you spoke with your rep? What did you go over last?

14. When was the last time your rep did a rate plan analysis? Who handles your wireless needs and purchasing at work?

(Note: When asking these questions, the best salespeople get a prospect to talk about the negative impact of their situation. They ask, "What frustrates you most about ...?" Or, "What do you estimate that costs you in lost time?")

THE FIRST DATE

It's important to have enough of these first appointments every month in the high-activity sales process. First appointments lead to quotes and quotes lead to sales. The right levels of each of these lead to sales and income goal achievement. Do them well and you will create greater prosperity for you, your family, your customer, and your company.

A final note to remember. If a prospect admits a need, want, or problem and wants to see a presentation, AND you need preparation time, then *schedule this presentation appointment before leaving the first appointment.* Doing this makes you more efficient and improves the opportunity ratio from first appointment to presentation. This tip will increase your sales productivity. Do it.

Chapter 12

PIED PIPER PRESENTATIONS THAT GET PEOPLE MOVING

Have you ever watched someone selling a high-energy blender at SAM's wholesale or tickets to see the five-legged sheep at a carnival? They draw you in. It's stimulating. Mesmerizing. Their greatness lies in their ability to capture your attention and then your emotions. They are the Pied Pipers of sales.

Have you ever been drawn into the proverbial fire like a moth circling a dancing flame? The pipes playing? The sirens singing? The fingers curling?

Years ago, I took my son to New York on his 13th birthday for his man trip. We went there to see the plays and to enjoy the time together. He is a sales guy like his dad and very good in artistic intuition and as a word merchant. In New York, we saw some of the best with word and wit in "Beauty and the Beast," "Smoky Joe's Cafe," and "Inherit the Wind." We feasted on the best pizza anywhere. It was a great trip.

As we walked down Times Square, I decided to show my son how to purchase a video camera and get a good deal. We walked into one of the many electronics stores in the area. Once we entered I don't remember much except being ushered back into the rear of the store by someone who smiled at my requests. I knew what I wanted and I knew the price I wanted. I was ready. I was a sales trainer. I trained sales trainers, managers, and VPs of Sales. I could handle the situation and my son would learn by watching.

It didn't take long. The music was low—the scent was in the air. I found myself pulling my credit card out of my pocket. The sales guy smiled. He talked. He smiled. He moved his hands. He moved me away from what I knew I wanted and to another camera that ended up in my bag. Out of the store. I was dazed. The camera was in the bag. Panic began to set in. I didn't want that camera. I bought it, but I didn't want it, and somehow I was outside the store.

Today, we laugh about it. I still don't know what happened. I remember looking for the courage to return, which I did. I mumbled something about buying something I didn't want. I remember the sales guy smiled. I was embarrassed, but I got my money back. Back out on the street. I didn't have a camera, but I got away. I'm one of the lucky ones. Many others bought that day and didn't return.

THE TELLING TIME OF PRESENTATIONS

While I do admire the skills of a carnival barker or someone selling a "slice-em-up Ronco slicing machine," I do not think this type of selling, using stimulus-response techniques, works well in long-term relationships. They do not help a high-activity salesperson understand the core of a person's needs, wants, or problems in a way that builds rapport and trust. They do not provide great referral strength and low rates of returns months after the purchase. **Those techniques do stimulate people into buying, but they do not bind them to the purchase, the salesperson, or the company.** And, as the complexity and size of deals increase, the demand for a quality approach to a sales pitch increases as well. For large deals, salespeople have to listen just to make the cut among potential vendors.

THE LISTENING CONNECTION

In the course of a presentation, you present a quote. What makes the presentation (that is, quote) to sales ratio higher? What makes the salesperson as a presenter credible and worth referring? The short answer is a person with an attitude of service and strong consultative skills. That means asking questions, listening, and presenting solutions. Effective salespeople who receive strong referrals give advice based on a clear understanding of a prospect's situation. They follow through and their product or service provides value relative to the price paid. When this occurs, referrals and good customer comments increase and improve the quote to sales ratio making the salesperson more efficient with time.

You might ask, "What are presentations about? Are they about my company's products or services?" No. **Great presentations are**

about the prospect. High activity sales professionals focus presentations on the prospect's situation with their wants, needs, or problems. *They focus their presentations on* **solutions** and those making the purchase know it.

Great presentations help a prospect see how the future will be better with the service or product being offered. Problems are solved. Wants are satisfied. Needs are filled. A situation with its negative impact—in dollars or frustration—is replaced with a positive impact of saving or earning dollars, or ending frustrations and gaining peace, pleasure, profit, or pride. The presentation helps a prospect believe a story that will help them release money to fund an investment. The story weaves together features and benefits in an explanation of reasoning and emotion that completes the decision process for a prospect. They decide to buy.

> High activity salespeople present standing up, sitting down, or walking across a client's property. No matter how they present, they stay focused on the prospect since it's their money, their time, and their decision.

To begin a presentation, summarize your understanding of a prospect's situation. Get agreement that you understand their situation. If someone wants to correct the notes you've taken, let them. If more than one decision maker is involved, this gives you and them the assurance that your presentation will cover the right things. With a large group, you can hand out your notes that outline these three (3) areas in a short one page summary: (1) Situation: Basic Facts and Information; (2) Situation: Needs or Problems; (3) Situation: Impact.

While presentations require time for telling, they also require time for listening to customer reactions and opinions and time to find out if there are any fears, questions, or concerns with a proposed solution. The entire presentation provides the facts, evidence, and information necessary to help a prospect make a good investment decision. Your closing ability will depend upon referral strength, rapport building, listening and presentation skills, proof, overcoming incumbent suppliers, achieving a satisfactory value versus cost comparison, answering questions and solving concerns.

High activity salespeople present standing up, sitting down, or walking across a client's property. No matter how they present, in different circumstances and settings, they stay focused on the prospect since it's their money, their time, and their decision.

THE TIE TO THE FIRST APPOINTMENT

What's the connection between the presentation and the first appointment? I've watched salespeople act like there isn't one. They just talk during the first appointment as if it were also a presentation. They do their best to talk about the things they believe will cause someone to buy. At times the customer tries to speak, only to find themselves interrupted by the rep. The first appointment for this type of rep is not a time to listen to the customer's needs, but to explain how a product or service works.

In essence, they seem not to care about the customer's needs and problems relative to their product or service. How do we know this? We know, because their presentation does not connect to the prospect's situation. Why? Either the first appointment does not contain a questioning time exploring a customer's situation, or the salesperson didn't listen, or the salesperson doesn't understand how to connect customer needs with their product or service.

When a salesperson takes the time to ask questions and listen prior to giving advice or solutions, their presentation sounds both convincing and familiar to a prospect. That's because a salesperson weaves into their explanation the adjectives and verbs they heard the prospect use when discussing their situation. If the presentation time occurs hours or days after gathering information, then the salesperson uses the notes they took on that day. At the presentation, the prospect hears familiar issues, times, people, places, or parts of their life or business in context with a need or problem area and its solution.

For example, a wireless rep, Maria, talks about how Bob can use a new MiFi connection to access the internet while away from home on one of his many training trips. Bob hears about how this new connection will make it convenient for him to get his emails attended to before he gets home. Maria explains that Bob, instead of staying up late at night after the return home, can get into bed with work completed and his mind at peace.

While showing properties to Laura, his prospective purchaser, Jeremy, as her realtor, can picture the need for the extra bedroom and recreation room Laura wants, and also remember her desire for a fireplace to snuggle next to during the cold winter months. Jeremy can also empathize with the home Laura is leaving, with its inadequate storage space for a growing family. Then he can present properties and the property features that satisfy Laura's needs. As Laura listens and ponders the connections to her needs, she is reassured by the understanding that Jeremy shows interest in her needs and problems while explaining the solution.

A home remodeler, Mike, walks around the space to be rearranged, and after listening to homeowners Jason and Mitzi, he explains how their need for better flow from the kitchen to the dining room will be constructed. And, after listening to their work schedules and the future events they have planned, Mike discusses the steps to completion and how they will meet their budget, timing needs, and space requirements. He also helps Jason and Mitzi picture the newly created space with family visiting and guests laughing and milling about as they enjoy their time together.

In a perfect sales environment, we hear the high-activity sales professional using word pictures to tie together needs and solutions. In the solutions presented, we hear concerns turned into peace, financial losses turned into profitable gain. This occurs as the professional asks and hears about the current situation and then explains how a product will fix the problems or satisfy the wants.

When a customer experiences a negative impact that's bringing frustration to life from either losses in property, money, or emotions, the high-activity sales professional who analyzes these well presents an alternative picture, one that brings a positive impact and more certainty to the future. Wow! That's how a salesperson creates referrals as needs meet solutions during presentations and then are made real by a product or a well-delivered service.

THE SIMPLE TRUTH

Why don't salespeople listen, really listen, and then, if appropriate and true, work to connect the needs and wants of a person with product or service benefits? Why, instead, do they glide into well-honed recitations of a stimulus-response message—one that seeks to control us and get us to buy through psychological positioning and through a calculating stimulus of our impulses? Why do they learn to say this if we say that and do this if we do that just to keep us fixated until we sign an agreement or say yes? And, why do some just spread their products before us without any further effort to listen to and attend to our needs?

The simple truth: They don't care.

Why?

It starts for us in the crib and continues in the family and at school. Move, wiggle, and motion to others to get noticed. Be the center of attention. Fight for recognition. We start early learning how to get our way. Also, most of us have never experienced someone really interested in our needs, someone who truly listens to us. So, how can we possibly know how to care about the needs of others and then talk in their best interests?

It is possible. We can change. We can learn the interpersonal skills for long-term relationships. We can learn how to listen to people for their benefit. We can learn how to ask questions, listen, take notes and then work hard to explain ourselves in a language that influences someone to buy. We can learn to sell with integrity.

Integrity is deeper and wider than honesty. If you look the word up, it means something that has all its parts. You can count on it. For a salesperson, integrity is like a four-legged stool. One of the legs is honesty. Another is listening. The third is product knowledge and presentation skills while the fourth is follow up after the sale. It's the second and fourth legs that are often missing and cause the salesperson to lose integrity in the eyes of a prospect or customer. Both of these legs require questioning and listening skills.

When the listening leg is cut in half or missing, the salesperson can still be an honest salesperson presenting products or services well. They are just without integrity. Why? Because the salesperson presents products and services well and in an honest manner but does not connect them to the needs of the customer. People don't like this and even think salespeople are dishonest. They want someone to understand their needs and to explain the product or service with their situation with its frustrations or pain in mind. They want someone to listen to them before offering a solution.

In my previous story, the salesman in New York had no interest in selling me the video camera I wanted. Most probably he had a vested interest in a higher commission if I purchased another product—one in which I knew little about the pricing. He was well armed with techniques for changing my focus and getting my excitement moved. As a result, I purchased something without rational connection to my needs and later suffered from buyer's remorse. The result. I took it back and talked about my negative experience with the store.

Contrast this with purchasing a term life policy from an insurance professional. I remember the time and attention he gave me while asking questions and paraphrasing my needs and desires. Later, after the purchase, this same professional followed up with me for years at Christmas, birthdays, and other events. The end result; I gave him referrals and I did not change suppliers even when future clients in the same industry approached me for my business.

An important question to ask during the follow up is, "How's the _____ (product or service) working when you _____ (insert what need or problem was to be solved)? Asking this question shows concern for customer satisfaction. Loyalty tends to follow someone who focuses their skills on the needs of others—someone who asks questions and listens during and after the sale.

BE DIFFERENT

There are many honest salespeople in the world, but very few with integrity. The leg missing—listening while asking questions focused on wants, needs, and problems.

Presenting honest product information in a persuasive and perhaps authoritative manner, while at times effective in making a sale, does not lead to strong referrals and loyal customers in the same way that honest and authoritative directions without listening doesn't endear you to your children.

Most salespeople just talk. They just play the pipes, turn on the sirens, entice with the flames, or let the customer choose from a menu.

However, that's not you. You will be different. You will learn to listen. You will listen to your children. You will listen to your friends. You will listen to your family. You will listen to the significant people in your life. You will listen to your prospects. And then, when you present, people will know you heard them. This will make all the difference. You will develop customers for life. The effectiveness of your first appointments and presentations will increase. Your ratios will improve. And, if you can actually be a person that cares, you will not have to fake it.

For now, fake it if necessary. Just learn the skills because it will help the numbers and your relationships with a prospect, a child, or a significant person in your life. Later, you just might even learn to love others better through these new habits. I did. And it's made all the difference in how I present myself through my words, my intent, and my actions.

Chapter 13

WHAT IS SUCCESS TO A CINDERELLA MAN AND WOMAN?

In the movie "Cinderella Man," we see the fighter James Braddock losing everything during the depression until he's living in a basement apartment with his family. Once a promising pugilist, perhaps a contender, he gets beaten by lower class fighters often called bums until he becomes one of the bums, too. The boxing commission pulls his license and puts him on the streets. Each morning, he stands in a crowd and struggles to get the attention of those who choose men for work on the docks that day.

At home, milk is stretched by mixing it with water. A slice of bologna is spread among five. Finally, as lights and electricity are turned off, Braddock's wife sends his children off to stay with a relative. In anguish, with his pride all but gone, James goes on public assistance (welfare), and then walks to Madison Square Garden to beg money from the bankers and promoters who used to earn their dollars off his fights. He does this to get his lights back on and his children returned.

I want to ask you this question. Was James Braddock, at this time in his life, a success? The answer is "Yes."

Why?

He was a success because he was giving all he had, his very best, for the benefit of others. In my opinion, that's all a person needs to do to be successful. Your best may not be enough to get the results at the moment that you need them, but it is enough; and more than that, it's what's needed if you are ever able to attain what you want.

You may ask, "What does this have to do with sales?" Hang in and I'll explain. I believe the explanation makes all the difference in goal-achievement in sports, in life and in business.

WHAT I'VE NOTICED IN SPORTS

For thirty years, I played or coached baseball. While a hitting instructor, I noticed that many young men would approach the plate in fear, especially in moments of great importance to the team. By this time in their life, how they felt and thought about themselves in performance moments seemed to be a reflection of: (1) What their parents (primarily their fathers) told them; (2) Reactions of others; (3) Previous results.

Giving their best effort had no effect on their self-image. Interesting. Only results or what others thought mattered. As their damaged self-images looked at situations confronting them, I saw them lose resolve and even decrease their intensity level. Some even quit altogether while standing with a bat on their shoulder and hoping for a walk to first base. Many struck out just watching the ball without changing the bat position.

I saw players unable to recover from a single strikeout. Others, a minority, were not affected by multiple strikeouts. The lack of production just seemed to fuel their desire to hit the ball and strengthen their belief that things would eventually change.

I've seen baseball players get a needed hit in the last inning after going hitless throughout the game. I've seen basketball players launch a three-point shot without fear in the closing minutes of a game and help the team win. I've seen salespeople walk in just one more door and make a sale after days of rejection. I've read about mothers giving up food, while trapped under the rubble of falling buildings, to save a child and at the same time lose their own life. I've known men to lose their lives while trying to save a fallen comrade in arms. I believe the same definition of success is woven into all of these examples.

YEARS OF ASKING

I've stood by a flip chart in the last twenty-five years with thousands of salespeople and sales managers asking this question: "What is success?" I also gave them these directions: "Wait before you answer. Picture that you have your eleven-year-old daughter or son in front of you. What would you tell them? Remember, what you say will have a profound impact on them for the rest of their lives. Now, please answer the question, 'What is success?'"

Here are the top four answers I receive.

1. Happiness
2. Personal satisfaction
3. Achieving a goal
4. Doing my best

These answers, while plausible and important, are no different from what Hitler or Saddam Hussein might have said. I'm sure Hitler wanted to be happy. He certainly wanted the Aryan race to be supreme even if it meant genocide for six million people (goal achieved). And, he did his best to satisfy his desire to get it done. No. All of these answers fall short.

After studying coaches with three major championships or more, I discovered that most of them defined success as **"Doing your best for the benefit of others while striving to get better each day."**

John Wooden, with 10 national championships, never talked to his players about winning. He believed that practice, effort, and teamwork were all that mattered. "Success is peace of mind which is a direct result of self-satisfaction in knowing you made the effort to do the best of which you are capable. The main ingredient of stardom is the rest of the team."

What that means to a salesperson or a sales manager is to do your best for the benefit of your family, your prospects, your customers, and your co-workers. If you're a part of a great company, these will not be in conflict. They will compliment each other.

Face fear. As I heard long ago, fear is usually just an acronym for "false evidence appearing real (I think Zig Ziglar used to say this)." Fear can be a false self-image you carry as a result of how you learned to view yourself and your performance. Shake it off. Get up there and SWING AWAY. Get around people who believe in you. Catch that belief and then throw everything you have into what you do.

IS YOUR BEST GOOD ENOUGH?

Don't confuse activity with giving your best. That's what this book is about. Are you giving your best effort at achieving the right levels of the right activities with the right people? Are you striving to learn from your mistakes and to get better every day?

> YOU ARE NOT RESPONSIBLE FOR RESULTS. You ARE responsible for the effort you give toward achieving them.

Reality. Your current best may not be good enough for the results you want by when you need them. That shouldn't cause fear. It should, however, make you change something. What can you do? Look for advice. Learn new skills. Increase your first appointment levels. Get out of the work you're in and find another opportunity in which to put your best efforts—one that works for you. Educate yourself. Grow.

WHAT ARE YOU RESPONSIBLE FOR?

Here's a startling statement. **YOU ARE NOT RESPONSIBLE FOR RESULTS. You ARE responsible for the effort you give toward achieving them.** When a baseball player walks to the plate he is responsible for effort at doing his job for the team. Salespeople are responsible to the prospect, co-workers, the company, and to those for whom they provide. But anything can happen. The economy may tank. Weather may not cooperate. A world war may start.

Think about people trying to survive after Katrina or the honest people who worked at Enron. Remember 9-11 and the firemen pulling bodies from the rubble 24/7. Nothing is certain and we cannot control outcomes. That's an illusion. We can control our attitudes of honesty, hard work ethic, personal responsibility, perseverance, self-control, a positive spirit, etc. We can attempt to do what is best to do, what we believe will achieve goals.

So, do what you can. Fight well. Learn to do things with more efficiency. Focus on the process. Practice. Learn the skills for sales planning, activity management (lead generation, prospecting, setting and holding appointments, doing presentations) and face-to-face interactions.

While you do what you can to get results or achieve goals, remember that you are not responsible for results but for the effort that goes into achieving them. When you see your numbers, do not let them devastate you. Embrace reality and work hard. Let the fact that you are not winning make you work harder at learning the sales process and how to use its tools and gain its skills.

Interestingly, this slight adjustment in thinking improves goal achievement. It helps to remove unproductive amounts of fear, criticism, perfectionism, and control. It can do this for you and it can do this for the people you lead.

INSPIRATION—KNOWING THE WHY BEHIND WHAT YOU DO?

So, how do you motivate yourself toward a best effort and making yourself better? How can you keep moving when your situation is difficult? What will keep you focused on the most important activities without being overly self-critical, controlling, or fearful? Here are three starters.

1. **Work on your character**. Develop those parts of yourself that make you a better person. Read biographies of people you admire and whose stories inspire you. Strengthen or gain beliefs about the traits of excellent human beings. Some of the more important traits that you will find include: integrity, service, work ethic, personal responsibility, teamwork, and perseverance (that is, completing tasks or projects from beginning to end even in the face of adversity). Ask people important to you about your strengths and weaknesses as a person. Learn to be different—better.

2. **Build a team** of people around you who want to pursue excellence in sales or coaching salespeople. Preferably, get around people who have or are pursuing the character traits you want to possess in greater amounts. Find someone or a group whose presence moves you to give your best. Grab a book whose contents will help everyone and study a chapter together each week.

Apply specific actions and skills during the week and talk about how the practice worked out in real situations at subsequent meetings. Continue this week to week until you finish the book. Do this with others. You can also practice like this by yourself.

3. **Find a cause**. When it's the armed forces, we fight for our country, our buddy beside us, or people who need protection. Great people realize life is an adventure and there are battles to fight and people to rescue. Perhaps it's the plight of the homeless that moves you, or the poor, or someone who's being bullied. Or, maybe for the first time, you act out of a sense of thankfulness and concern for your customers. In many training sessions, I've asked salespeople, "What's the first thing that needs to get better in your life relative to money, something that MUST change and get better over the next year or two? In the movies, when a gun is laser focused on a target, you see a red dot on that target before the gun is fired. What are you laser focused on achieving? What's your "red dot" want or need? Is it related to a person or group of people? Can it become a cause?

Years ago, while training salespeople on goal achievement, I had everyone tear apart magazines taking pictures and visuals related to the important things in their life. Each rep using what they had found created a poster with a collage of their vision for the future with its dreams and wants fulfilled. When the presentations began, a young lady, at that time a single mom, shared with us her desire for educating her daughter in a specific private college. After that day, her production increased. Year later, I discovered that her daughter did, in fact, attend and graduate from that college. Her mom focused for years on that single cause.

What's yours?

AT NIGHT

When we motivate ourselves to success, it's about lying down in our beds at the end of the day knowing we gave all we had toward the accomplishment of important goals that save, protect, and provide for or help people. That's the great salesperson, sales manager, business owner, parent, friend, son or daughter, etc. We motivate ourselves to success each morning as we get up and remember who we are, the value we bring, and the people we fight for. We are "Cinderella" men and women without fluff or pretense. We know who we are, what we stand for and why.

Now, let's go and make things better! We can.

Chapter 14

ACTIONS STEPS—LEADS AND APPOINTMENTS

You can change the sales results you get by focusing on the process or the steps leading to them. This begins with lead generation—finding the right people to approach and prospect. This is like searching for buried treasure. It requires you to intertwine strategy, hope, and courage into a high-activity sales professional's work habits.

Our sales strategy begins with determining the characteristics of an ideal prospect. With that description in hand, we look out to the markets, locations and best places to search. As leads flow in, we make decisions regarding their priority by comparing them to our ideal prospect characteristics. Then we choose the best leads as prospects to call for first appointments.

This means you develop your own lead generation engine with different channels of work output which will power the engine into producing the quantity and quality of leads we require. Being independent in this way keeps you from being dependent on the company's lead generation. In retail settings, the store is a channel for leads and prospects and first appointments occur as you work the floor. While receiving these leads from store traffic is a good thing, high-activity sales professionals do not wait on them. They work to build their own lead sources from referrals, old customers, and other activities. You will not hear them say, "I wish the company would advertise more. Nobody is calling wanting to buy," or "Sure is slow today." The best salespeople in a fast-moving sales cycle do not have time to talk about slow traffic. They are too busy producing leads, prospecting, and holding appointments.

For business-to-business sales, you generate your leads from lists, referrals, trade shows, networking groups, cold calling, and in many other ways. Sometimes, sales occur at an initial meeting while other sales require several appointments to close. Usually, the sales cycle is less than 90 days.

Remember, calling time is fundamental to setting appointments. Schedule it on your calendar. You must spend enough calling time to produce the right amount of first appointments for yourself. Those of course lead to presentations and quotes and sales.

Begin your presentations with a summary of a prospects situation with its needs and problems. As you continue, speak about the use of your products or services within the prospect's own story. This presentational approach shows you heard them and it lets them experience how the use of the product or service in their world makes it better, more satisfying or profitable or creates a more predictable future. Even at this point in the sales process, listen and ask for reactions and opinions regarding your advice. Allow feedback and concerns to surface, acknowledging their validity and then helping with more appropriate advice, reinforcement, or answers.

As you do the planning and action steps in the lessons in Part II, Leads and Appointments, you strengthen your ability to get results. Now, here are a few actions to remember:

1. Decide your lead generation channels.
2. Begin to attend the events, join the clubs, or put together the lists.
3. Fine tune your lead generation to look for target profile prospects.
4. From the leads and lists, develop a prospects-in-progress list that contains the names of companies or individuals you will approach for first appointments.
5. Schedule and protect time to set appointments.
6. Set enough appointments to meet your "first appointments held" goal. (Realize that the right levels of the right activities with the right people lead to results).
7. Draw out the needs, problems, or wants of customers. Take notes. Paraphrase your understanding of what was said.
8. Close the deal with a presentation during the first appointment, or like the sales process for many sales teams, at a subsequent appointment.

SUCCESS TIPS TO REMEMBER

Remember, success comes to those who give their best effort for the benefit of others. Your responsibility lies in a hard work ethic to keep the right activities at right levels. Results flow from the Right Levels of Right Activities™ (the sales process work) and the quality of your interactions with prospects.

Success, giving your best for the benefit of others, has more to do with values and beliefs and corresponding attitudes than it does with techniques. Who are you? What do you stand for? Asking yourself these questions is another way of saying, "What are your standards?" Knowing the answers to these questions makes you stronger and less uncertain. This improves your influence with those you sell to, those you sell with, and the company for which you sell.

> Success, giving your best for the benefit of others, has more to do with values and beliefs and corresponding attitudes than it does with techniques.

What is your purpose when selling? What is your dominant motivator? Is it solving problems, filling needs, creating value? Is it making money, beating others, or being recognized? Can there be more than one dominant motivator in sales? No. There can be many important ones, but only one most important motivator for the role of sales itself. What's yours?

What character traits do you want to exhibit in your life? What will you do to practice these and make them a part of your nature? How will the traits you choose affect sales goal achievement?

▼ ▼ ▼

Focus on presenting solutions to the needs, wants, and problems of prospective customers. Work to create a positive impact with people, customers, and co-workers, as you strive to reach sales goals and income levels. You can do this. People depend on you. Do it.

Part III

MANAGING ELEPHANTS, ANTS, RIVERS, AND ACTIVITIES

One morning I shot an elephant in my pajamas.
How he got in my pajamas I'll never know.
GROUCHO MARX

Chapter 15

MANAGING A SALES FUNNEL— FROM LEAD TO SALE

had the following conversation with a sales team I was training recently. The team was behind in sales, revenue, and margin goals year-to-date.

Our conversation started with, *"What's the goal?"* They asked, *"The sales goal?"* I nodded. Each person quickly and rather smugly announced a year-end sales goal. I wrote their answers on a flip chart.

Most sales teams do not know their team goal or their year-to-date progress toward its achievement. Even more telling, most salespeople do not have goals.

I then asked, *"What are your year-to-date sales?"* Without hesitation, each salesperson responded with a number, their confidence growing with every answer. I continued to write. Actually, this interaction was impressive. **Most sales teams**

do not know their team goal or their year-to-date progress toward its achievement. Even more telling, most salespeople do not have goals, but that's a story for another time.

I then looked at them and asked, *"At the bottom of your sales funnel, how many quotes are pending (the number and $ amount), and one more stage up in your sales funnel how many prospects do you have that have not yet been quoted (the number and $ amount)?"* They responded with silence and confusion.

I explained, *"I want to know the number of quotes still viable and awaiting a decision and how much revenue they represent. Do you know these numbers at this stage in your sales funnel?"* Silence. *"Then, I want to know how many qualified prospected deals you will be given an opportunity to quote and the estimated revenue they represent. Do you know these numbers?"* Silence. More silence and, some shook their heads no, while others formed and softly said the word aloud, *"no."*

I continued, *"Those numbers are just as important as sales-to-date, perhaps more important. Why?"* One salesman in the group ventured a guess, *"Because knowing the number of pending prospects and quotes waiting on decisions will tell us if we are finding and working enough potential deals to achieve our goals by the end of the month or quarter."* I reinforced his answer, *"Yes, and if you know how much is presently in your funnel, you also know if, in the time remaining, you have a prayer of achieving your goal!"* At this point in the training, everyone was beginning to nod and a coaching "ah-ah" effect had entered the room.

▼ ▼ ▼

FUNNEL MANAGEMENT QUESTIONS

OK. Let's act like you do know your goals and you do keep track of your sales-to-date each day, week, or month. What are some questions about your funnel management for which you might not have ready answers?

To arrive at these questions act like it is the fifteenth of the month. What are your sales month-to-date? How many new prospects have you found? How many first appointments have you held? How many presentations did you do? *Were all these at the right levels?*

As you come to the end of the month, do you know if activity has been high enough for your sales production to continue at levels high enough to reach your income goals? Can you quickly identify the most promising sales-in-progress for the next period's income? Can you analyze your closing ratio, percent of sales from referred leads, and how well you choose who you prospect, that is, first appointment to quote ratio?

Do not feel bad if you can't quickly answer the questions. Don't. Ninety percent of salespeople cannot answer these questions, so most work hard each day oblivious of what is necessary to make mid-period corrections to sales goal achievement. It's usually too late by the time they see that they will end the month short of goal.

How do you manage your activity level when you are so busy working hard at all the duties of a high-activity sales professional? How do you keep critical sales activities (CSAs) at appropriate levels all the time?

FUNNEL STAGES

Managing a sales funnel begins with defining its stages and getting everyone on the same page with terminology. Here's a rather standard description of a three (3) stage sales funnel:

Stage One—**Prospects** is the top third of the funnel. It contains those lead prospects or opportunities as yet undefined for needs, current funding, or for when the buyer wants ownership to begin (installation schedule, purchase, etc.) For leads entering this stage, a salesperson has not yet been in front of a buying influencer with a first appointment in which the above items are discovered.

Stage Two—**Activities** represents the middle third of a sales funnel and contains those opportunities in which a first appointment occurs with a decision maker. A salesperson also learns about the needs, situation, funding, and schedule of the pending purchase. The rest of this stage contains subsequent appointments and advances that win the ability to quote and that occur before giving a final presentation and quote.

Stage Three—**Sales-in-Progress or Quotes** contains all deals presented and still pending award to you or your competition. A final presentation to a decision maker(s) usually advances a prospect into this quoted stage.

Sales flow out the bottom of this typical sales funnel. To easily remember this as a process, simply memorize that **"The Greatest Salespeople in the World Manage with PASS!"** (Prospects, Activities, Sales-in-Progress, Sales).

> *The Greatest Salespeople in the World Manage with PASS! (Prospects, Activities, Sales-in-Progress, Sales).*

A few notes to remember:

1. Teach everyone on your team the descriptions for each stage in the funnel. Change the names if it's helpful.
2. Be aware that the amount of time that a lead flows through the funnel, top to bottom, *ranges from 5 minutes (a fast wireless sale) to 90 days (typically less than this) or beyond.*
3. Understand that the *opportunity ratio* is the ratio of first appointments to quotes. If there are too few quotes occurring from first appointments held, then prospecting strategies or face-to-face skills may need to improve.
4. Discover your *closing ratio, the* ratio of quotes to sales. It's another area for possible improvement and training.
5. Find out your average size and source of sales. You may find you need to quote larger sales, and increase your referrals.

VARIOUS FUNNEL MANAGEMENT METHODS

The simplest method I've seen for funnel management is a **yellow pad** of prospect names. As they are worked, top salespeople cross them off. After first appointments are set and held, if prospects continue down into the funnel, then quoted amounts are placed by the name. These are known as sales-in-progress, an inventory of deals working, and by other names. Check marks and dates are placed by a deal that closes. A quick glance at the yellow pad at any time allows a person to know where they are during the month relative to goal. It also displays what deals might close by the end-of-month or carry over into the next month. Along with the yellow pad, these top salespeople use a simple to-do list for managing important tasks.

SPREADSHEETS

Over the years, I have helped sales teams stay on track with various tracking systems. These range from simple excel **spreadsheets** to online management funnels. As a result, if moderate to great talent was present, I most always saw increases in productivity. For those who needed to find other employment, the tracking helped everyone make that decision sooner than later.

In the spreadsheet category, across the top, I have placed columns for the Critical Sales Activities (CSAs) by category with their activity level targets in separate columns, one for actual and one for targeted levels. This flowed from left to right from prospects found, appointments held and set, to quotes and then sales produced. The spreadsheets were laid out left to right just like a sales funnel flowed top to bottom. Separate tabs represented each month. After Google started allowing shared spreadsheets and documents, it was a no-brainer to

144

use its online storage area for the teams I coached. It has been extremely successful as a shared tracking tool. With it, salespeople update their activity and sales numbers prior to weekly sales meetings.

CUSTOMER RELATIONSHIP MANAGEMENT (CRM)

There are many online CRMs on the market. Many of them will allow you to categorize a prospect's position in the funnel. IT personnel develop most of these. However, many high-activity sales professionals do not like them. These reps work fast and do not want to slow down for management's need to accumulate data regarding customer interactions. Because of their complexity and the time necessary to keep them updated, many salespeople regard CRMs as a type of black hole of time actually impeding sales progress. CRMs are not developed to help high-activity salespeople work a process that teaches them to keep critical sales activities high enough to help them achieve their income goals.

ONLINE ACTIVITY MANAGEMENT

With my business partner, Steve Suggs, a former Northwestern Mutual representative, I recently developed another type of online application to help salespeople manage sales activities to reach their income goals. *SalesActivities.com is an online sales funnel with precalculated levels of sales activities necessary to manage a needed flow of sales and income.* It's also simple to use—like the yellow pad.

SalesActivities.com contains a sales funnel organized to keep you doing enough critical selling activities to reach your goals. It makes sure you work enough prospects, set and hold the right number of first appointments, and get enough quotes out each month to meet your goals. And all this is pre-calculated to your average sales size and closing percentages.

SalesActivities.com was designed to help manage the *Right Levels Of The Right Activities*™ to reach income goals. It also helps reps manage flow through their sales funnel. As another benefit, reps can see and better manage what's in the funnel. This results in a better system for improving sales goal achievement.

BENEFITS TO FUNNEL MANAGEMENT

When you use a yellow pad, a spreadsheet, or an online funnel management application like **SalesActivities.com**, its constant use will help you:

- Hit your activity levels by tracking them against your targets.
- Smooth out the peaks and valleys and roller coaster sales.
- Focus on qualified prospects and strategies to win sales-in-progress (quoted deals).
- Learn to produce more accurate forecasts.
- Make better strategic prospecting adjustments earlier in the goal achievement period.
- Keep new lead generation at an appropriate level.

All these contribute to higher income, lower selling expenses, and greater sales efficiencies.

Manage a sales funnel and coach activity levels and strategies that place enough new customers into Stage Four, **Sales**. You can do this. Do it.

Chapter 16

EATING AN ELEPHANT ONE BITE AT A TIME

Elephants are big at birth, perhaps 250 lbs.; full grown, 10,000 lbs. or more. I'm not sure of the origin of the metaphor in this section's title. But it helps to understand a truth within the world of a high-activity sales professional.

Steve Suggs, a well-accomplished sales professional, says that achieving a year's sales goal is like an elephant. It's big. How do you attain it? "One bite at a time." You break the goal into monthly and weekly amounts. You turn those smaller goals into a specific number of presentations or quotes, first appointments, and prospects.

You then work to "eat" this year-end goal in bite-size amounts. Each week, you remain consistent with prospecting activities, appointments, and presentations at the right levels. Keeping these critical sales tasks at calculated levels leads to healthy sales goal attainment per day, week, or month. It helps to smooth out the peaks and valleys, feast or famine in sales production.

CONSISTENCY

In life, we strive to be consistent with our commitments and with what others we respect say is right and true. We like fairness and its application in commissions earned and benefits given. We want a grading system or a sales board to be consistent in its treatment of each rep's sales results.

I don't know about you, but my wife likes my paychecks to be a consistent amount she can count on each month—an amount that's consistent with our bills and lifestyle goals. I remember, years ago, I used to get home and walk up smiling about a potential new account in the funnel. I would say something like, "Wow, if this closes, it will give us this amount of money!" It didn't take long after just a few deals fell through, for her to ask me for a check. She wanted to know what to count on, not what "might be." Today, I don't even bother talking about deals in the funnel. I have learned it's more important to bring in a consistent income (deposited checks) than celebrate over potential deals.

WRITTEN GOALS

We tend to act in a way that is consistent with the commitments we make in our lives. Some psychologists measured the change in attitude people had after making a bet on a horse. Before they placed a bet, they appeared nervous and uncertain. After they made a commitment with their money, their confidence rose in their picks to become consistent with their betting commitment.

When we write down a goal, and then give it to others as a declaration of our commitment, this should cause us to act consistent with, or in a manner that represents, that position. However, I think this falls short of where we should focus. If we are truly not responsible for results, and it truly is more important to focus on the process rather than the goal, then we should commit to specific levels of critical sales activities: prospects found, first appointments held and presentations made, or quotes delivered.

So, what are your activity commitments? Where are they written down?

CONSISTENCY

The origin of the word "consistent" comes from a Latin word in the late 16th century and literally means "permanence of form." Its meaning depicts something that holds together or stands firm. When we think about a sales funnel, one that produces consistent sales, we see a flow of sales like a river with the funnel serving as the riverbanks, giving it form.

In the eastern part of Tennessee there is a river I know well. Years ago a dam was placed on that river by the Tennessee Valley Authority to generate electricity and control flooding in the region. A great trout fishery exists in the river tail waters below the dam. Anglers wanting to fish those waters need to be mindful of the inconsistent levels of the river produced by the dam's controlled generation that changes flow according to rainfall patterns during the year. A danger exists for the fishermen as the water sometimes flows very strongly and sometimes stands still in pools with quiet ripples. Interestingly, when fishermen fish in the river several miles downstream and the generators cease at the dam, it can take hours before these fishermen detect any change in flow.

It's the same way for high-activity sales professionals. When prospecting occurs upstream in the funnel and first appointments are completed at high levels, fishing is strongest at the bottom of the funnel, where many quotes are being produced and sales closed. This is a time many salespeople start paying attention to the fishing downstream and stop the consistent flow of or 'fishing' for new prospects. Depending upon the levels within the funnel at that time, a lack of sales will eventually be detected downstream. The problem occurs when salespeople are so caught up in the activities surrounding pending deals that they stop lead generation. Even one big deal can cause this "big deal-itis." Sometimes, it's 30 days or more before they detect a lack of pending sales. Then, it's either too late or almost too late to get the river of prospects flowing to catch enough fish (sales) to eat for the current month. This is a problem all salespeople have experienced: feast or famine, food on the table or threat of starvation.

The solution is to keep lead generation and prospecting to minimum levels all the time. Dedicate consistent time to this area of the sales funnel. To accomplish this, some actions taken by high-activity sales professionals include:

- Track the number of new prospects, appointments set, and appointments held.
- Keep lead generation and appointment calling hours as scheduled time.
- Hold prospect meetings at their office.
- Limit prospecting to a certain geographical area as much as possible.
- Hire support staff for other noncritical sales activities and tasks.
- Push necessary paperwork to support staff or to hours late at night.
- Work 80-hour weeks until support staff or marketing people can be hired.
- Schedule the amount of time spent at customer or prospect meetings.

BACK TO ELEPHANTS

When you look at elephants from a distance they don't look all that big, especially if you are sitting in an air-conditioned building as part of a circus audience. But, change your vantage point. Walk out among them in their native environment as one lone person standing on the ground. This will change your perspective and you will gain a greater appreciation for their size.

Let's break our elephant—the yearly sales goal—into bite-size chunks.

Except for leap years, a year is 365 days. Weekends take away 104 possible days for sales production—leaving 261 days. Another 10 days is removed for vacation. And, 10 days are removed for holidays and sick days. This leaves 241 days. So let's say we have approximately 240 days for sales production in a year. This means we have 20 working days per month. 20 x 8 or 10 hours per day = 160-200 hours. What will you do with these hours? How many hours will a first appointment take? How many first appointments do you need to set and hold each month to generate enough quotes and sales for your lifestyle's income needs?

BITE-SIZE

As you look at the average size of all your deals and the time available each month, you may need to close more revenue per deal to make it all work. What that will mean is changing your ideal prospect definition to one that can produce a higher deal size. Then, you will increase your average revenue per sale. A financial services rep might begin to prospect higher net worth individuals. A training consultant prospects only mid-size companies with 100+ salespeople versus small businesses with 3-10. An insurance professional now only approaches companies with 500 or more employees. In all of these examples, you will find people working just as hard and with the same number of appointments, but they have changed their sales results to consistently higher levels.

What is the average size of your deals throughout the year? Or, what will they be?

Your answer will make a difference in determining activity (quote) levels for consistent income production.

ELEPHANTS AGAIN

As the year progresses, remember the elephant eating metaphor. It is certainly possible to eat something large over a certain period of time. But, if you stop eating, if you stop the consistent and constant work at it, you will be faced with a time trap—not enough time left to achieve the goal. Usually, you will not catch up. You will not have enough time left to get enough prospects, first appointments, and presentations in place to get the results you want.

Some salespeople hope to close "the big one" and even get big deal-itis hoping for and working toward one mega deal to the detriment of "bread and butter" average size deals. This is a recipe for poverty, as well as indigestion.

▼ ▼ ▼

You can be consistent with the most important sales activities. I want to help you with this. We can do this together. Let's do it.

Chapter 17

RECORDING ACTIVITY AS IT FLOWS—DAILY

Someone once said, "Consistency is better than occasional greatness." St. Francis of Assisi, a great man of charity toward the poor, wisely advised:

1. Start with what is **necessary**,
2. Then do what is **possible**,
3. And suddenly you are doing the **impossible**.

For a high-activity sales professional, it is **necessary** to prospect and to set and hold first appointments **at the right levels**. Make this a consistent habit. Do the right number of first appointments per week and month and record progress.

YOUR NUMBERS

For many years, as a baseball hitting coach, I kept statistics, and I did the same for sales teams I coached the last 25 years. After every game, I ran the numbers—at bats, walks, hitting percentage, hit-the-ball ratios, on-base percentages, strike outs, etc. Why?

From these numbers, I designed practices to make the team better. One player worked on a particular skill while another worked on something else. In the four years I coached high school baseball, every team batted above .300 and we usually had 2 batters batting above .400. If you're not familiar with baseball, batting averages at or above .300 are what the major league players shoot for, and are rare indeed for teams to average. On my teams, each player knew his performance level and the process steps to take both mentally and skill-oriented to improve.

What are your numbers? Where do you keep them? What simple method do you have to measure the key performance indicators that propel you to your sales and income goal?

STANDARDS

All great teams and industries have standards. In the sporting world, baseball has a standard of above .300 for great hitters. In football, a great runner compiles a 1000-yard season. Basketball players who score greater than 20 points a game are great scorers. There are practice standards for these teams as well, to improve their physical conditioning, free throw percentages, batting averages, and other important parts of the game that lead to wins at greatness levels.

People run businesses to meet a profit standard each year. Depending upon the industry, these profit margins may range from 4% on up. Businesses carefully record sales, cost of goods, and expenses because of competition or tight gross margins on products sold. Those businesses which do not record cash flow and expenses steer themselves with undirected emotions and dangerous decisions.

Tracking your numbers allows you to compare yourself to standard norms in your industry or company. These comparisons can both help and harm you. Obviously, the way they help is by letting you know where you "stand" relative to what is thought to be average or great performance. Then, you will have a rallying point, an authorized standard to shoot for. However, this may limit your thinking and your sales performance to those norms. You may think this is the area of the possible and not think or behave beyond these levels.

RESULT STANDARDS

Let's start here with some important questions. What sales results do the greatest salespeople at your company or in your industry achieve each day, week, or month? (As the sales cycle lengthens, these numbers are more important at monthly levels rather than daily levels.) How much revenue do they average or how many widgets do they sell? How many sales do top salespeople close each month?

Now that you know what great looks like by the numbers, what does average look like? How much revenue exists in an average sale or how many widgets? If you are an entrepreneur, see if you can find industry statistics for these numbers, perhaps from peers in noncompetitive areas or from your trade or industry association. If you are a salesperson, ask your sales manager about the results that average versus top performers achieve. Having these will help you determine activity levels leading to your sales and income goals.

ACTIVITY STANDARDS

What are your standards for critical sales activities? By knowing these, you will know if you are doing a quality job with activity management. What are great activity standards in your industry for appointments per day or week, presentations (quotes delivered) per day or week?

As a consultant or lone entrepreneur getting started without company records, why not create standards, number of appointments or quotes per month, and then work to lift them? Then, as your business grows, you can lead and teach salespeople you hire.

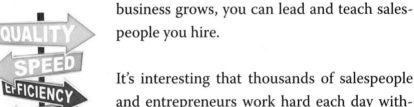

It's interesting that thousands of salespeople and entrepreneurs work hard each day without any measurements further upstream of results. For that matter, some businesses do not even know what their monthly profit and loss statements or cash flow look like.

What problems do you think having no record of the past causes? How does this affect knowing what you will "stand" for as a minimum or best level of productivity?

HISTORY

George Santayana was a philosopher, essayist, poet, and novelist. Here's what he said about history:

> "Progress, far from consisting in change, depends on retentiveness. When change is absolute, there remains no being to improve and no direction is set for possible improvement; and when experience is not retained, as among savages, infancy is perpetual. **Those who cannot remember the past are condemned to repeat it.**"

We don't want to remain infants in what we do. We want to mature and a good record of our history will help us be accountable to the change we want in the future. If we record our results, we can look back and see progress. We can see failure. We can see the activities that worked and the ones that did not. We can see lead generation methods that produced for us and the ones we need to remove from our engine.

When we keep our history in some kind of permanent form, we can see how our previous behaviors and skills brought us a certain performance level. When that history includes a record of sales activity levels leading to results, we can improve the process, the steps leading to results.

A NEW DISCIPLINE

Have you recorded activity in the past with a yellow pad, a spreadsheet, or an online application? **Have you tried to use one of the new CRMs on the market? Did it help you keep your activity levels high enough for goal achievement?** Were you consistent with keeping it up-to-date or did you begin to fall behind and wonder what's the use? If you didn't keep the activity up, the reasons why likely included that you:

- Were not sold on the benefits—especially that it would help you increase your income.
- Believed it was a way for management to look over your shoulder.
- Did not understand the relationship between critical sales activities and results.
- Could not find a CRM that tracked levels of critical sales activities.
- Were not encouraged to keep up with logging and recording activity.
- Received no training to show you how the system would help you make more money.
- Found the tool too complex to use.
- Did not see your results change or your income rise.

If these touch on any of your reasons for complaining about CRMs or not keeping the data up in them, then I think you've got a point.

The purpose of this book is to help you earn more income through better activity management. That said, I want you to sell yourself on managing activity by testing the ideas in this book. To do that, please do the exercises I ask of you. Do the actions I list after each chapter and sections in the book. Understand the simple math behind the critical sales activities necessary for your sales goal achievement. Correspond with me on **CoachSalespeople.com, SalesManage. com**, or **SalesActivities.com**.

I'm not interested in looking over your shoulder. You don't need that. You may need someone to challenge you and to give you good advice. That I will do.

I want you to learn to increase your activity to levels that help you eat well. I want you to do enough lead generation, prospecting for first appointments, and quote production. That's it. If I can help you accomplish this and teach you how to do this yourself, the results with take care of themselves.

Learn about the relationship between activity and results. High-activity selling industries have magic ratios.

Learn about the relationship between activity and results. High-activity selling industries have magic ratios. For example, "see 10—quote 3—close 1" is a standard in some financial sectors. **You also have a magic ratio.** Discover what it is and open yourself up to greater achievement.

Use a spreadsheet or use an online application like **SalesActivities. com**, which helps you set and track levels of critical sales activities. CRMs have several useful bells and whistles for customer relationship management, but what you need is something that helps you record activity levels, measure them against target levels, and follow prospects from lead generation to sale. Then, you will have enough customers to need a CRM.

I want this book and what I do to encourage you to learn activity management as an important skill area. This will help you be self-supportive and enable you to translate these abilities to whatever high-activity sales position you may accept. Be encouraged and excited about this self-improvement sales training and that I know you can achieve marvelous increases in your income.

▼ ▼ ▼

In sports, all types of critical statistics are kept: batting and on-base averages, pass completions, free throw percentages, etc. These numbers are recorded to understand the effectiveness and efficiency of players and play. These statistics help focus practice on specific skill improvement. They tell when to use different game strategies. In many ways, key performance numbers help teams improve their play and win results.

As a part of our activity management process, with its tools and skills, we want to help you learn to record your activity. Why? Because, then you will know if you are holding first appointments and other important activities at the right levels. Remember, first appointments lead to presentations or quotes, which lead to sales. There really is a magic ratio in the match of your activities even if you do not know it is there. Search it out. Learn what it is. It will make you learn what it takes in activity to be a higher paid professional.

▼ ▼ ▼

How many first appointments did you hold last month? How many presentations or quotes did you give? What is your closing percentage? How many pending sales remain in the funnel?

Know these answers. Then the truth will set you free. Free to grow and get better.

Chapter 18

KEEPING SCORECARDS AND SCOREBOARDS

Whether in golf, bowling, baseball, or any other sport, what's the purpose of scorecards or scoreboards? That's easy. To display the score, right? Yes, and to see the time remaining so that everyone understands who is ahead and what it takes to win the game. On most scoreboards, we find other important game-specific numbers that impact results like errors and hits for baseball. Fouls, timeouts remaining, and time remaining on the shot clock appear on a basketball scoreboard. Football scoreboards, like the others, also show the score and time remaining, but they also contain the yard line, down, and yards remaining for a first down. During any of the games played in these major sports, spectators and players alike can see the scoreboard and get a feel for who might win.

What is your favorite sport to watch? Now, picture sitting in the stands watching a game in which your favorite team is playing, but

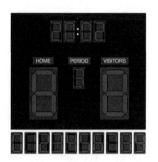

you cannot find a scoreboard anywhere. What difference would it make to you or those watching? What difference would it make to those playing the game? How would this affect the coaches?

You play the sales game, don't you? Doesn't it make a difference for you when you do not see a scoreboard (sales board)? Where is your scoreboard and how often do you look at it. And what numbers does it contain other than sales-to-date, your , and the time remaining? How do you know if you have a chance to win?

HIGH-ACTIVITY SALESPEOPLE—HOW THE BEST THINK

Years ago, I began to observe top high-activity salespeople and how they manage themselves to hit their goals. Where do they keep their prospects? How do they monitor their goal achievement progress? How do they track where they were in relation to their goals?

Here's what I learned. All of them carry some form of a prospect list, a holding place for leads to be prospected. Somewhere, in their head or on a piece of paper, they carry a list of sales-in-progress, a list of those decision makers who want a quote or have one and are trying to make a yes or no decision.

I saw these top reps chasing sales and the deals most likely to close. Sometimes daily and certainly each week of a month, they ask themselves a question. "What are my sales results month-to-date?" As they think about that number, they subtract it from their goal and realize the answers to three more questions.

1. How far am I from my goal?
2. How much time is left?
3. What sales do I have working that can close by the end of the month and get me to my goal?

Top salespeople run these questions and their answers through their heads continually. They manage these realities every week. Their thoughts are like a sales board that they carry in their heads or create on the fly with a pencil and piece of paper.

The motivation behind their thinking varies. Some reps compete to win and gain recognition. An absolute amount of money to be earned for specific uses (savings, debt, play toys, basic living expenses, etc.) keeps the attention of other great reps. Competition, financial reward, and recognition, along with a specific personal responsibility are the most often observed motivations of reps leading teams. They think about their month-to-date progress for motivating reasons. Those most often at the top of the sales team know what they want, why they want it, and they think about their chances of getting IT (their specific want).

Do you think like this? You probably do if you have an intense desire for an "IT."

SALES PROJECTIONS

High-activity sales professionals make projections, but not in the way they teach in textbooks. They do not make 25%, 40%, or 62.5% projections. These don't make sense to them.

Instead, as they run and gun through the week, all they want to know is: "What am I ninety-five percent (95%) sure will happen by the end of the month?" They arrive at that number or projection by taking their actual sales-to-date and adding the deal revenue (or total widgets) they think they have a 95% chance of closing by month end. Then, if they are half way through the month and they are at 60% of goal, they celebrate and keep pushing. If they are at 40% of goal, they kick themselves in the place that gets them focused on that part of the sales funnel most important for catching up and reaching goal by month's end.

THE IDEAL BOARD

I decided to create the ideal sales board based on how top reps think and on how critical sales activities drive results downstream. I wanted to create the best representation possible of a top rep's thinking in a way that would be simple, easy-to-understand, and use. I did not want 5 or 10 stages in the funnel, only three, the critical three, and in some cases, for some companies, only two.

Using the columns of a spreadsheet, it would contain an actual month-to-date column and month-end goal for the following:

(Columns for Critical Sales Activities)	(Column for Results)	(Column for Forecast)
• Prospects found • First Appointments held • Quotes presented	• # of Sales • Amount of Sales Revenue (widgets, if compensation is based on number of units sold)	• 95% month-end Forecast

These columns were designed to run left to right from prospects found to sales just like a sales funnel flows top to bottom. A logical flow. By using this board every week, a rep could train himself or herself to keep the critical sales activities flowing and to keep track of month-to-date progress to goal achievement. The ideal model would reflect the productive life of a high-activity sales professional.

PERSONAL CUSTOMIZATION

Currently, different types of organizations use boards we at Sales-Manage Solutions have designed. Some use **SalesActivities.com** online. While prospects found, first appointments held, and quotes presented are universal sales terms, some organizations like to customize the terms to fit their culture. Some organizations call prospects leads. Others call first appointments new appointments. Quotes may be called presentations. Sales may be expressed in fee amount or revenue or widgets. To me, what's most important is that everyone agrees on the definition of each stage of the funnel and to keep it simple and clear. Also, it's important to minimize the number of stages and create a sales board that is useful and easy to keep up.

PUBLIC AND VISUAL

Make sales boards public and visual. For sporting events and sales teams, there's no difference between why players and spectators alike need to see a visual representation of progress. Scoreboards and sales boards help everyone understand how much time is left and what it takes to win. If sales teams meet for a weekly sales meeting, place the board in a prominent position. It's interesting to watch the effect of a well-designed sales board on a team's productivity. Placing the board where all can see it during the sales meeting has a positive effect. It actually lessens the amount you have to say in a sales meeting. Peer influence permeates the room. Those on the bottom of the board do not have to be told about their position or their need to improve. It's all visible and in the light.

PERSONAL REACTIONS

I've seen various reactions to sales boards. Some salespeople quit before they are fired. It's just too painful for them to see their lack of results, skills, poor work ethic, or lying made visible to everyone. Reps can't lie to the board. If someone reports more first appointments than they held, then quotes are too low. If quotes are reported too high then sales are too low for reasonable closing rates. It's easy to see something's amiss when using a well-designed board. A sales manager can always drill down under the numbers to explore what's happening.

On the other hand, high-performance sales professionals appreciate the wisdom of continually knowing where they stand. Consultants, financial advisors, wireless reps, security sales reps, and thousands of other reps work each day to keep the flow of prospects and quotes high enough to reach their monthly goals.

One reaction to seeing sales numbers made public can be shame or self-condemnation. This is a reaction that great coaches handle with care. As we grow up as young men and women, we are taught to see ourselves through how we appear to others. Many reps are sensitive to criticism. A coaching tip to remember, "Never call a rep out for poor results in the middle of a sales meeting."

For all lone entrepreneurs and companies with any number of reps, a visual sales board will help analyze performance and keep you focused as you work your 80-hour weeks. Put the board where you will walk by it often. It will amaze you how looking at the board on your way in and out will help you with your sales performance.

ONLINE SALES BOARD

Use a spreadsheet or online application like **Salesactivities.com** to help you keep a weekly sales board that shows how activities lead to results. The board will show you how you're doing toward hitting targets for key activities: prospects, first appointments, quotes, AND then sales.

By knowing in real time where you stand, you can then make adjustments. I am not talking about a board that shows only sales results, but a board that shows the activities that lead to results. That will make the difference. Instead of pounding on yourself for missing results, you can focus on improving parts of the sales process—or the activity level leading to results.

You can improve sales results by activity management. Keep a weekly sales board. You'll know what you currently don't know. This will help you have more fun, more sales, and more income.

Chapter 19

ANALYZING PROGRESS AND MAKING IN-FLIGHT ADJUSTMENTS

Picture in your mind the beautiful banks of a strong river. It flows over and around the rocks and into the quiet pools of an exquisite and peaceful lake. This body of water in which the river empties lies healthy and vibrant because of the great stream that feeds it. People enjoy the fishing, the sun, and beauty of its clear waters.

Over the years, I've enjoyed fishing in many streams and lakes in the USA. Some of these fisheries and boating paradises have not continued to remain healthy and, recently, fishermen have not found the same bountiful harvest of years ago. Even the boating has been affected by the change in water conditions and the once simple pleasure of the past is now in the past, unavailable for present and future generations.

I'm sure there are many reasons for these changes in lake conditions. For some of these expanses of water, the rivers that fed them were no longer attended to and the housing and manufacturing that grew up alongside them changed the stream quality (results) downstream.

There are many systems that must be attended to upstream of results to continue producing a future we will like. Likewise, in business there are systems that must be maintained in various "upstream" areas: operational, service, financial, profit and loss, and sales goal achievement, in order to preserve and protect the health of the company.

When we pay attention to the upstream actions that lead to results like lead generation, prospecting for appointments, presentations and their activity levels, we are able to make adjustments. We make these intelligent changes in time to cause a remarkable and positive difference downstream on future sales periods and their results.

THE INSPECTION

Working for the benefit of others is a virtue, however working without tracking progress may not lead to prosperity. Working smart means we must think about how we do what we do. Many salespeople do not think about how to make themselves better. They do not analyze the process by which they accomplish their results and thus do not know how to improve themselves. When salespeople inspect what they do, ideas emerge to free them from unproductive behaviors, attitudes, and beliefs.

I propose to you this action. Schedule a specific time in the first three days of each month to sit down and review the past month's results—what worked and what did not. Examine each part of your sales funnel in detail. Then do this with your peers, the salespeople you sell with, if that is possible. At a minimum, go over your activities and selling strategies with someone you respect. In this inspection time, brainstorm what happened that was good, what happened that was bad, what remains , and what is missing regarding your sales performance and goal achievement finish. Look at your answers and seek to discover a set of adjustments to make in the present month. Write these down. In subsequent months, evaluate whether these adjustments were made and how they contributed to positive change.

REMEMBERING THE PROCESS

To make an inspection that leads to a good improvement plan, remember the sales planning steps you focused on in the beginning of the book. Also, remember the critical parts and ratios in your sales process. It contains elements and steps upstream of results. Beginning at the bottom of the sales funnel, I've listed the following areas and related questions to consider in your inspection.

* **Income goal** and uses of income or reasons for achievement. *Are you dedicated in your heart to its achievement? Really? Why? Do you have to earn this income or achieve this level of sales? Why? Final questions: Do you believe you can achieve it?*

Do you believe your products or services help people? Honest answers to these questions tell you if your achievement drive is high enough to accomplish your goal.

- **Sales goal** in revenue or units per year, month, week, or day.

- **Average revenue** or number of units per sale (estimate).
  Did you estimate the right number as an average in your initial activity calculations? Missing this number on the high side can cause you to close the number of sales you wanted but not produce the revenue or widgets sold to obtain the commissions you want.

- **Number of sales** per year, month, week, or day.
  Of course, this is calculated based on your sales goal and average revenue or widgets sold.

- **Ratio of sales to quotes** (estimate of what is commonly referred to as **closing ratio**).
  How effective are you at getting sales to close and did you set a realistic target for this ratio? Obviously, if you estimate a closing ratio that is too low, then you will not meet your sales target. To improve this number, generate leads more closely aligned with your ideal profile of a customer. Also, work on your face-to-face sales skills and follow up.

- **Number of quotes** per year, month, week, or day.

- **Ratio of quotes to first appointments** (what I call the **opportunity ratio**).

  How often do your first appointments end up in a presentation or one at a subsequent appointment? This is a measure of prospecting the right leads and the quality of leads produced. This ratio can also be affected by the number of referrals you receive verses other types of referrals—your referral strength.

- **Number of first appointments** per year, month, week, or day.

- **Number of prospects found** per year, month, week, or day.

  Is this number high enough in order to have enough prospects to work on for first appointments? Are you consistent at finding new prospects each month at a pre-determined level?

- **Target customer profile** and description of a great prospect.

- **Lead generation methods** and marketing channels.

  Have you described an ideal prospect well enough to target people or companies matching your description? Are your lead generation methods worth the investment of time and money? For example, if you have one, is your leads group worth your investment? Certainly, yearly and perhaps more often, an inspection of lead methods and marketing channels can redirect your energies to more appropriate lead sources.

Do not keep doing the same activities if they do not produce the results you want. Do an inspection monthly, quarterly, and yearly.

THOUGHTS FOR A HIGH-ACTIVITY ANALYSIS

Look over the inspection described above. At a macro level, are you doing the Right Levels of Right Activities™ with the right people? First and foremost a high-activity professional is ACTIVE at the highest priority sales activities—prospecting and appointments. For a majority of working hours, the best reps are either in front of a prospective customer or fighting to get in front of one.

At pre-determined levels,

1. Find new leads.
2. Set and hold first appointments.
3. Conduct presentations or get out the quotes.

If you are new to activity management, start here. Do these activities at the right levels.

Burn this thought into your head—**RIGHT LEVELS OF RIGHT ACTIVITIES.**™ Increase your activity level with new prospects. You can then make your self more efficient and effective. You may even be able to decrease your activity and get the same sales results.

Do not love on prospects for too long. In the same way, do not massage a big deal (called big-deal-itis) so much that you lower critical sales activities and put future revenue in jeopardy. Major in bread and butter size deals which have a faster sales cycle, less complexity, and less customization required in quotes and presentations.

ATTITUDES AND BELIEFS

How you think about yourself, your product or service, your company, co-workers, prospects, and your customers restricts or propels sales goal achievement. While the purposes of this book are more related to the tangible behaviors and activities you do, I want to explain some crucial forces weighing heavily on your goal achievement.

Your philosophy with its attitudes and beliefs powerfully directs how you approach sales work and problem solving. For a moment, let's explore three areas and their effect on activity management.

Rate yourself 1-5 (1=low and 5= high)

Self

Do you like yourself?
Do you believe you can get the job done?
Do you think you are worthy of a six-figure income?

When someone dislikes themself or works with low self-confidence, this has both negative and positive effects. While it may drive someone to gain recognition, it may also bring instability to their prospecting, activity levels, and goal achievement when someone doesn't approve, reacts negatively, or isn't positive toward something they attempt or do.

Confidence in one's abilities brings less stress and anxiety into the day and improves energy levels. It also improves how others respond to a sales approach provided it isn't accompanied by arrogance and doesn't remove the focus from the prospect.

To lessen income self-sabotage, those who grew up among families or in cultures with lower incomes may need to work on seeing themselves at higher income levels. Reaching six and seven figure incomes, with the associated work ethic and responsibilities, requires personal growth and a change in belief and attitude.

Work

Do you enjoy sales?
Do you respect the company you work for?
Do you believe that your products and services help people?

Important research shows that 55% of salespeople should be doing something else. What if a bricklayer or surgeon should be doing something else? Would that affect the job they did for you?

Make sure you are in the right role. Sales personalities usually have a high social drive and confidence and a high need for results in short periods of time.

Are you proud of the company you represent? As this attitude lessens, so does achievement drive and sales power. If you disrespect the company you sell for, then leave. Your incongruent feelings for the company you represent will make you less effective in going head-to-head with competitors.

In the same way, it's important that you believe the products and services you represent will fulfill their promise and create value in the marketplace. (That's a fancy way of saying that they will help those you serve and they will provide a fair exchange for their investment. Otherwise, unless you're a charlatan, you will not be able to look someone in the eye and lie forever.) Believe in what you sell or sell something else. Value rendered in the marketplace affects your activity levels and your confidence in front of prospects.

Future

Do you like goals and goal-setting?
Do you desire to meet each period's sales and income targets?
Do you believe your life will be better in the near future by your efforts?

Since every 31 days high-activity salespeople start over with their goal achievement, the best ones love goals and goal setting. They drive themselves through competition, a need for recognition, or for the excitement of achievement alone.

Outstanding sales professionals want to meet their numbers. As a result, you will see them track their progress and want to know where they stand. It's the money accumulating, the sales accumulating, or their name at the top of the board that fuels this desire.

If you score a perfect 45 (1-low, 5 high) on these nine questions, giving yourself a five for each one, then your achievement drive is high. Since achievement drive is the multiplier of your skills and abilities, its strength is most important in getting high-activity sales results to great performance levels. When activities are not meeting targeted levels, and sales are low, and your inspection finds significant improvement areas, also check your beliefs and attitudes.

Sometimes skill problems can be traced to inappropriate attitudes and beliefs.

MAKING ADJUSTMENTS

As you work your plan and record progress, you can look at the numbers to analyze progress and make adjustments. Just like a pilot flying from Miami to New York, you can check your dashboard for important course corrections. The pilot works through a checklist of questions designed to understand the progress of the plan and make necessary in-flight adjustments. You will do the same thing with planning questions designed for high-activity sales goal achievement.

You can improve by focusing on the parts of the sales process "upstream" that require you to be more active or to strengthen your skills. You can make adjustments during the year to the sales plan, sales activities, or people skills that you believe will get you back on an income and sales goal achievement track.

▼ ▼ ▼

I want you to reach or exceed your goals. I want to help you know how to find the training and tools for better sales productivity and its high income. I want you to do the *Right Levels of Right Activities™* for a better lifestyle.

Chapter 20

A GREAT ROLE MODEL— THE ANT

It's hard to find a great role model in today's politics, business, sports, or families. It's hard to find someone who remains consistent with their standards of excellence, someone who does not waver but acts constant in behavior, productivity, and professionalism.

Why? Why is it difficult to find an advisor who will model standards for us that will help us long-term in our profession? Let me offer a few possibilities:

- Breakdown of the family and lack of parental presence or a trusted authority.
- Lowered morals in politics, business, and culture
- Teachers and coaches who are easy on students and players or focus only on results

- Lowered graduation, military entrance, or educational standards
- Lowered standards in many parts of our society and culture
- Easy rewards for those who refuse to work
- Promoting people without leadership qualities into management roles.

Do poor advisors or a lack of guidance keep us from becoming better? Maybe. But maybe it's our fault. Maybe it's our own depth of character. Maybe we're choosing not to work hard or persevere during difficulties or try new activities with courage and discipline. Maybe we choose to do what's comfortable when what it takes to achieve requires pain or extreme effort. Maybe we stop working at 40 hours a week when entrepreneurs put in 70-100 hours every week for months. Maybe our will to win is weak and our resolve wavers in times of struggle.

Whatever the reason for a drop in standards and character strength, it's tough to find a mentor or sales manager who sacrifices for the long-term advancement of another.

So, let's turn to nature to find the perfect role model for high-activity sales professionals. And there we find the Ant. Yes. The Ant.

 Aesop wrote "The Ant and the Grasshopper." It's a fable about the Grasshopper who sings lazily throughout the warm summer months while the Ants consistently store away food. During the following winter, food is scarce and the hungry Grasshopper turns to

the Ants for help. They properly chastise him for singing away the time.

Moral: Time is money and food. Put your time into the activities that pay and feed you.

THE ROLE
High-activity sales professional.

THE SALES CYCLE
90 days or less. Perhaps, a few sales have longer cycles but they are not the norm. Each month the sales period and efforts start all over again. Like different horses are bred for different functions, you'll find that excellent salespeople race. They do not plow.

What are some other role models for high-activity salespeople?

OTHER ROLE MODELS
Racecar driver
Around and around and around they go fighting for position and racing for the flag. The clock is running and an exact number of laps remain. Danger looms. Wrecks occur. The yellow flag brings caution to the race. The money and the trophy and the fans await the winner. Paying attention to the details at the start, in the turns, in the pit, and at the finish gives an edge to the winners. Pit stops, yes or no, wheels off or wheels on. The best drivers approach the track with courage and take calculated risks to get them ahead and to the finish line first.

Bricklayer

Time is money. Bricks not laid result in not being paid. The clock is running. The owner is waiting. To get food on the table, you finish the job on time and under budget. After you finish, it's on to the next job and another tight schedule. An apprentice learns from the master craftsman who teaches the young bricklayer how to toil, get along with others, and take pride and satisfaction in a job well done.

Greyhound

The prize, the prize, the hare just out of reach and just ahead. Keep striving, keep reaching, and keep focused on the moving target. Until it's over, until the next race, and it all starts over again. The racing Greyhounds pace at very near 40 mph. Wow. Do you run fast and on the right track to win the race? Do you want something with so much intensity that excitement courses through your veins and you cannot take your eyes off the prize?

Are you like these models of high-activity? Do you push yourself to get ahead before half of the month is over: 50% done and 60% of goal? Celebrate and keep pushing! Pace yourself. Push yourself. Make it happen. Keep running, keep racing, keep setting those bricks (appointments), and chasing the prize.

SALESPEOPLE WHO ARE ROLE MODELS

In the last 30 years, I have watched the best salespeople consistently sell the most. They also received most of their sales from referrals. Most of their past customers were repeat customers. These great reps had the greatest customer satisfaction and the highest performance.

If being at the top of the sales board does not mean someone is the best salesperson, what does? Customer satisfaction, low returns, brand protection, and referral strength factor *combine with high* sales to create a long-term and valuable sales impact. Top reps who sell in this way do not lie, or give poor follow up, or communicate poorly with buyers. As a result, they are much more profitable with time spent selling. The results on sales productivity from this customer-centered approach are:

> *Customer satisfaction, low returns, brand protection, and referral strength factor combine with high sales to create a long-term and valuable sales impact.*

- Reduction in time required for lead generation and prospecting
- Increase in quotes from first appointments
- Increase in sales from quotes
- Shorter sales cycles
- Higher margins

Please look for or be a mentor who models the service attitudes that create strong customer relationships. From models like that, you can catch the attitudes and beliefs of a high-performance sales professional who is respected and even revered by those they serve.

A GREAT INSTRUCTOR

We can watch interactive teaching occur in life around us. One teaches another and behaves as a role model for necessary life activities. We see this in the world of ants. One ant interacts with another to teach the companion how to find newly discovered food. One slows down to help the other and shows sensitivity to the learner's progress.

Solomon describes the Ant in the book of *Proverbs* as a role model for consistency in work. *"Go to the Ant you sluggard; consider its ways and be wise! It has no commander; no overseer, no ruler, yet it stores provisions in summer, and gathers its food at harvest."*

What does the Ant say to us? Get to work. Stay at it. Provide for those you love. Do your duty. Be consistent. Do the *Right Levels of Right Activities*™ *each and every sales period. Prepare for winter and continue to eat well even in tough times.*

▼ ▼ ▼

I want to help you smooth out the peaks and valleys of sales performance. I want to help you keep prospecting, holding first appointments, and conducting presentations (presenting quotes) at the levels necessary to maintain your chosen standard of living. I want to help you with the learning, processes, tools and skills which will make this a practical reality. I want to help you be better than you are today.

Chapter 21

ACTION STEPS—MANAGING ACTIVITIES

On September 11, 2001, Todd Beamer, a passenger on United Airlines Flight 93, realized through an in-flight phone call the ultimate plans of the hijackers on board his plane. All of America remembers his famous words, "Are you guys ready? Let's roll."

It was a hero's call made from someone going about the business of the moment. While the passengers of this flight did not make it home that evening, they did not allow the terrorists to accomplish their objective. They did their job. They stopped the terrorists.

When the plane lifted off the runway, the passengers thought this flight would be like any other. Business men and women worked on their laptops. Parents and those around them persevered through the crying and arguments of children on board. Stewardesses made sure people were buckled in and their carry-ons stowed overhead or under seats. When the terrorists took over, the intensity and excitement increased and Todd and the others got ready to roll and to do what was necessary to take the terrorists out.

FUNDAMENTAL

To finish this part of the book, "Managing Activities," I thought about Mr. Beamer and the other heroes and heroines on Flight 93. While all of them were traveling with different agendas, when the moment came to choose the activity of greatest importance they chose to act and we are forever grateful. Today's high-activity salespeople, and what they do, cannot be elevated in purpose to Mr. Beamer and friends. However, great salespeople always find the sacrificial route to follow for the benefit of others. They realize their purpose as company catalysts—the sparks that cause something to happen between a new customer and products and services.

As high-activity salespeople consider their role in the profit and loss statement of the companies they work for, a sober thought occurs to them. If someone doesn't sell enough products and services, their company will go out of business, people will lose their jobs, and bad things will happen. This lack of action will affect administrative, manufacturing, installation, and all other types of employees. In a high-activity environment, everyone works to take care of new and existing customers; and, as existing customers leave for various reasons, new customers replace this lost revenue and keep companies from losing ground.

When high-activity salespeople take a step into the world on any workday, it's important for everyone that they sell enough to support the revenue needs of the company. They may or may not sell for some high purpose or to satisfy customers. Oftentimes they just want recognition, someone to compete with, or a chance to achieve or earn the money. Whatever the reason, many have to be reminded about activity levels. They need a coach. It's easy, even for high-performers, to get lost in minor activities that do not lead to results.

ONE BITE AT A TIME

If your activity plan shows 6 first appointments, 3 quotes, and 1 sale each week to meet your income needs, then remember this. Do 6 first appointments and 3 quotes or presentations every week. Elephants are big. So is a year's income. While there are 365 days in a year, do not think you can miss your activity levels for a few weeks and make it up later. When you begin to think about dropping your intensity, remember the old "Lost in Space" movie and the robot's words when a threat approached the young boy hero. "Danger, Will Robinson, Danger!" Do not get caught up in big deals or non-critical activities. "Danger, Danger!"

RECORD ACTIVITIES

Write down your activity targets and your actual levels of them each week. If your plan says 6 first appointments and your actual is 5, record these numbers. Use a yellow pad, a spreadsheet, or an online application like **SalesActivities.com**. Gradually, you will build a history of results and ratios and you will begin to play in the big leagues where records and variables leading to great year-end performances are understood by a history of recorded progress.

Whatever you do to document your numbers, keep it simple. Do not spend more than 15 minutes per day using your system and do this work early in the morning or as the day concludes. Keep prime time available for critical selling activities.

VISUAL SCOREBOARD

Last year I began to use a Moleskin notebook to record every important note and my various to-do lists during the year. It was a combination journal and note-taking storehouse. As I began to think about how to keep track of my weekly walking as a physical exercise target, I decided to use my Moleskin. On the last page of it, I drew 12 vertical lines. Since the notebook was already ruled horizontally, I put 1-31 down the left side. Each of the now formed columns represented a month and each box formed by the horizontal lines represented a day. It was now easy to record the number of miles walked each day and tally it for the month. I loved it. So simple and it worked.

I later adapted this chart for sales reps at a wireless company. In the math of their activity model, if they found 6 opportunities a day they would sell 100 handsets a month and earn in excess of $85,000 per year. For these wireless reps, some of their opportunities (first appointments) walked into a retail store setting. By recording their actual number of opportunities a day, they realized how many opportunities they needed to find outside of the store through other lead generation channels. Recording the number of opportunities found and the number of handsets sold each day was easy with this simple chart. The chart's visual relationship between activities and results got them calling old customers and getting out of the store to find new opportunities. Sales increased.

Make something work for you and be sure to include the critical activities that lead to results. For most of you, simply label the columns in your chart with the number of prospects found, first appointments held, presentations made (quotes delivered), and revenue or widgets sold.

ANALYZE PROGRESS

What do college football coaches do after a game? Watch the film. What do ships' captains do? Keep a log. What do quality improvement managers require? Records. Coaches, captains, and managers require a past view of process numbers upstream of results to make adjustments. Pilots make on-course adjustments through a flight to safely navigate a group of passengers to their destination.

High-activity sales professionals achieve sales and income goals by staying on track. However, to stop at times and look at the past may not be natural to them (or to you). Many do not have activities recorded and visual scoreboards. First things first. Find a simple way to record the critical selling activities, develop a chart, and then begin to establish a monthly planning meeting right after month-end. Any responsible pilot pays attention to wind conditions and weather and makes corrections for an on time and safe landing. As you analyze progress, make adjustments to reach your destination—your sales and income goal.

FIND A MENTOR

Pick someone who can understand what goal achievement requires in a high-activity sales environment. Do not pick them because they sell. Pick them because they are wise and you respect them. The right people might be just a little bit intimidating for you to approach. You might not feel comfortable around them because they will challenge you and tell you the truth. Do it anyway. Allow their challenge and perception to reach your ears and heart.

Show your mentor the activity plan you designed and your numbers year-to-date. Explain the sales funnel and how you manage its flow. Ask them what they see and for their advice. Even if you do not agree, listen. Do not react to their advice for 24 hours. Then, consider it again.

RESULTS

Finally, it's really all about giving your best toward commitments and goals —your income, your company's or your family's financial security. Do what it takes to win with integrity as you work with prospects and co-workers. Follow the money. Be intense and intentional about it. Prioritize who you spend time with and what you spend time with so that you spend the majority of your time doing critical selling activities. Focus on activities leading to results and make changes in their levels to achieve them.

In this part, Managing Activities, you focused on what it takes to manage the work of a high-activity sales professional. You worked to understand the basics of activity management. Consequently, you now know how to describe the sales process as a funnel with different stages and the critical sales activities that define them.

With a simple yellow pad, spreadsheet, sales, or an online application like **SalesActivities.com** as a tool, you can manage the necessary activities in a sales funnel. As you manage the *Right Levels of Right Activities,*™ you can also stay on top of sales-in-progress, proactively tackling the next steps to bring pending sales and a prospect's decision to closure.

By recording daily activities with leads and prospects, you create a history of sales activity numbers versus results. This helps you understand your previous standards. It gives you a basis for perfecting the sales process and obtaining ideas for greater sales performance.

Your weekly sales board shows current goal achievement progress. By seeing a chart of critical sales activity targets versus what you actually get done on a weekly basis, you keep from getting too far off course before making adjustments. You can then analyze how you use time, whom you spend time with, and your effectiveness at setting appointments and handling face-to-face sales calls.

In this part, we watched our role model, the Ant, work consistently to eat the elephant one bite at a time. Without a manager, the Ant manages time with prudence, keeping in mind that today's activities affect its future.

Guard the motivation of your heart. Do this daily. Keep at it.

I want you to earn enough money for today's survival needs and for your vision of tomorrow. I want you to prosper today and tomorrow. You can do this. I know it. "Let's roll" together.

Part IV

MANAGING A
SALES FUNNEL—
FROM LEAD TO SALE

*The spirited horse, which will try to win the race of
its own accord, will run even faster if encouraged.*
OVID

Chapter 22

RECRUITING A HIGH-ACTIVITY SALESPERSON

I remember my father preparing to go on "bow only" deer hunts years ago. At the back of our garage sat a small workroom he had built. In it, he stored things of interest to him: old radios, transmitters, fishing and camping equipment. My father worked as an electrical engineer and he organized his things in plastic boxes and cabinets. He believed in safety on the job. Going on a hunt with dangerous weapons meant, for him, safety first, then organization and the right tools.

As a young boy, I attentively watched each step as my father prepared his hunting equipment. He showed me two types of arrows— one made for practice with a rather blunt metal tip and the other made for hunting with a very sharp broadhead point and multiple cutting surfaces. Both of these arrows were dangerous in the hands of a boy. My father took special care to explain this to me. He saw the danger of uneducated hands notching an arrow into a bow string and randomly selecting a shot. I learned as much about safety as I did hunting by watching my father, an expert, at work.

▼ ▼ ▼

Some people do not handle a bow well or a business—especially when they recruit salespeople. Often, their poor judgment occurs because of a lack of experience or a lack of advisors and training. Entrepreneurs and small business owners make lots of mistakes when they launch and manage their business growth. One pivotal mistake made in the development of a small business occurs with hiring the wrong salesperson.

There may be some debate about King Solomon and the truth of his reign. However, for more than 2000 years people have read and studied words of wisdom ascribed to his authorship. His wise sayings found in the Bible's book of *Proverbs* prove to be true in application. About hiring, Solomon advises, **"Like an archer who wounds at random is he who hires a fool or any passer-by." (Proverbs 26:10)** Yet, each day an entrepreneur or small business owner does this. They hire someone and their choice is as dangerous as "hiring a fool or any passer-by." They do not know how to make a wise choice and later they experience the *negative impact.* Time, opportunity, and cash flow diminish. New potential customers choose another vendor. People even lose their jobs or their businesses because of a hire that's made with "uneducated hands."

BEST PRACTICE

Changes continue to occur each day in our businesses and for the customers we serve. Technology seems to move the world at an accelerated pace. Customers demand quality and timeliness. Customers know more about what they buy before they purchase. Competition doesn't rest and new sources of it seem to appear in unlikely places.

It's hard enough for us to keep up, much less bring someone else along, especially someone we have to drag along. In many businesses, 50% of new sales hires last only 6 months. To manage effectively, much depends on our ability to hire effectively! Great coaches sometimes get away with less than the best. And mediocre coaches win lots of games with great players when the one thing they do well is recruit! Recruiting great salespeople means finding people who pull the business along a profitable path with new and satisfied customers.

For several years, I researched articles and books on recruiting and hiring. The businesses that excelled seemed to recruit and employ the best people. From my research, I discovered that excellent businesses worked hard to determine if someone was suited for the company's sales team. Also, I saw a parallel between great sporting teams and excellent businesses. When several Division One schools recruited my son for a college baseball scholarship, it was evident that the best had a "system" for evaluation and others relied on "feel." Schools with winning traditions worked a system and pursued players with specific character traits, competencies, and personalities. They did not rely on feel or intuition. Best practices written for sales team recruitment also mirror the same systematic step-by-step approach we find working in great sporting teams.

WHAT TO LOOK FOR?

As I touched on earlier, important research shows that 20-25% of the sales force can sell, but should sell something else and that 55% of reps on most sales teams should be doing something else. What this means to you is that on average, 20% of your reps will sell 80%

of the business. First year production, retention, and overall team production increase when sales leaders recruit people more suited for the position. Go find the 20% who *can* sell what you sell and experience these benefits.

I have asked hundreds of sales leaders this question, "What do you look for when you hire a salesperson?" Less than 5% can describe the most important traits they desire in a high-activity sales professional. So this question occurred to me, "How can a sales manager recruit salespeople who will perform well if they cannot describe the top traits the position requires of them?"

Many sales positions do not have job descriptions that accurately reflect what a salesperson does. Sales managers, when recruiting, do so without understanding the selling **competencies** required beyond the obvious need to close sales. They do not know the **competencies,** or the **personality traits** and **character traits** necessary for the company's culture and a specific sales position. Competencies and personality traits in top performers do vary from one sales team to another while character traits remain the same. When sales leaders educate themselves and know what to look for, they tune their recruiting tools (screening questions, structure) to look for specific traits thereby increasing the chance to make a good selection.

Think about these questions when recruiting a salesperson. What about ramp up time? Do you want to hire potential? If so, you can look for those with the personality traits, but without the "street smarts" and then coach them! What attitudes are important to you and to this job? Independence? Service? Coachability? Honesty? What changes in the marketplace and company affect what you look for in a salesperson? And, how must a salesperson behave to face the challenges that the sales effort demands each day?

I'm going to provide you with my top list of character traits, competencies, and personality traits for a high-activity sales professional. While these apply to many high-activity sales positions within various industries, you may want to add or adjust them for recruiting a rep into your business. For further information and help with recruiting salespeople, please visit **salesmanage.com/blog**, or **CanTheySell.com**.

CHARACTER TRAITS

Did your momma ever say, "Birds of a feather flock together," or "We don't associate with people of spotty character"? Maybe not, but these sayings tell us to be careful who we bring into our lives and onto our sales teams. A salesperson can sell more than anyone ever has and put you out of business, limit your future business, or cost you a bunch of money in legal fees.

In his book, *Good to Great,* Jim Collins presents the research data behind a 5-year study conducted by 21 people. The researchers whittled down 1435 companies to 11. The 11 companies had 15 previous years of mediocre performance followed by 15 years or more of great financial performance. In their study, they isolated the universal characteristics of companies going from good to great and why some companies made the leap and other did not. When looking for employees, these great companies recruited character first.

I have identified four non-negotiable character traits for your sales recruiting and selection process. If someone does not show evidence of these traits during screening and structured interviews, do not hire the candidate.

1. Honesty
2. Hard work ethic
3. Personal responsibility
4. Servant-hearted

Two additional traits are optional for sales reps but mandatory for sales leaders:

5. Positive
6. Humble

1. Honesty: Great salespeople let their yes be yes and their no be no. Their words and actions are free of deceit and untruthfulness. People think they are sincere. They tell the truth to prospects, customers, and other sales team members. They get to meetings on time. They follow up. You can count on what they say. They treat people and situations with consistency. They are authentic and real in every sales and service situation.

2. Hard Work Ethic: Sales professionals put energy and effort into doing the right level of critical selling activities. They do this to achieve sales goals. They are free from laziness and believe that being lazy is wrong for them. They do not waste time with activities that do not contribute to the achievement of personal responsibilities and sales results. As William Shakespeare wrote, "Does thou love life, then do not squander time." Great salespeople do not misuse time.

3. Personal Responsibility: Dedicated salespeople own what they do and the results that occur. They steward the resources and duties surrounding an opportunity. They work as though they have a personal obligation in fulfilling their position's duties and its purpose. They do not hide from responsibilities. When being given a task, goal, or purpose to accomplish, they focus on its achievement as a duty. When you turn your back on these sales reps, they will do what you thought they would do and more.

4. Servant-hearted: People who are great salespeople see the sales process as a buying process that is adapted to the needs of the client or customer. When you watch them work, you see them perform duties for others with devotion and concern for their welfare. As a result of their service-orientation, sales reps provide customers with an excellent buying experience that lifts a company's brand and image, generates referrals and develops customer loyalty.

5. Positive: Sales reps also create value by how they focus what they say. The best ones center their words on the strengths of people and employers. They praise and encourage other reps. They talk about management strategies and important values like service and goal-achievement plans. They support their peers, vendors, and management with optimism, a benefit of the doubt, and a "can-do" attitude. This is an important trait for sales managers as well.

6. Humble: Outstanding salespeople (and especially sales leaders) have a modest view of their own importance. Because of this they can give away recognition. They thank people and point to the contribution of others. They share their strategies and techniques.

COMPETENCIES

Is a person already proficient at the main duties of a salesperson? That's a question you answer with a best practice selection process. (However, when hiring a young person with little experience, the past cannot predict present sales abilities. Their performance capability remains unproven. To improve a prediction of an unseasoned candidate's sales potential, you have to rely on their personality traits and look at profile assessments and their past to guess at their latent competency. This increases reliance on validated assessments that provide profiles through well-designed and well-structured questionnaires.) The following list of competencies depicts skills and mastery areas for the high-activity sales professional.

For each 31-day period, a great salesperson:

1. Finds enough leads to prospect.
2. Sets and holds enough first appointments.
3. Builds rapport by adjusting to different personality types.
4. Asks questions and listens to needs and problems.
5. Presents solutions and investments to individuals and groups.
6. Works through win-win solutions to a prospect's fears, concerns, and questions.
7. Asks for commitments, fulfills customer promises, and asks for referrals.

PERSONALITY TRAITS

A person's work ethic, practice, environment, and life experiences shape each of us from birth. Without getting into an argument regarding how much of our success is due to genetics and how much to culture, let's agree on the following: At any given moment, some people are more prepared to do one thing or another. For example, in basketball some will perform better as point guards, some as centers. Engineers with their set of personality traits build safer nuclear facilities while other people perform well in daredevil stunts in front of an audience.

From a personal perspective, one of my sons is analytical and possesses an exceptional gift of detail. One son can string words together well with great creativity and enjoys being around people especially in moments requiring persuasion. Another son likes to be outside, manage properties, and work with his hands. One is social; another prefers a small group of friends. Credit the reason for the differences to what you will. My bride and I brought them up in the same home, yet all three are gifted with vastly different and unique skills, tendencies, and preferences. One of my sons enjoys a high aptitude for high-activity sales. The other two do not.

During years of using validated assessments like Craft Profiles, **craftprofiles.com**, I learned that top performing high-activity sales professionals have a few core personality traits in common. When salespeople possess these traits, they experience less stress than others when doing the competencies of this position. These personality traits include:

1. Goal-orientation: a high drive for quick results; less methodical.
2. Social drive: a need to be around people; energized by people contact.
3. Social confidence: a tendency to tell others what to do (rather than ask).

Look at the competencies listed above, and visualize someone who does not have these personality traits. How will that affect their ability to continue to perform at high levels over an extended amount of time?

BEST PRACTICE RECRUITMENT FUNNEL

When researching recruiting experts, a best practice recruitment funnel emerges. The three stages of recruiting are: Screening, Profiling, and Interviewing. At each stage, look for evidence of the 4 character traits, 5 competencies, and 3 personality traits.

candidates

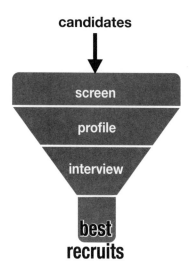

recruits

Recruitment Stages

Stage One—Screening: There are several ways to screen a candidate for necessary competencies and traits. They are: by resume, phone (5-7 minutes), face-to-face, references, email, etc. An interesting way to screen by email is to ask the candidate to send you how they plan to approach their first ninety days as a new rep.

Stage Two—Validated Profile: After screening each candidate, a few make it to the personality profiling stage which increases predictability for talent selection by as much as thirty percent (30%). A profile also provides an objective look at your candidate. I use the CraftSystems CPQ (Craft Personality Questionnaire @ **www.craft-profiles.com**) that has 30+ years of sales recruiting research and 4 million+ administered tests (see **craftprofiles.com**). From the profile, you will receive a high, moderate, or low job match and the personality trait scores within or outside of the acceptable range.

You will also know the type and amount of coaching that each rep will require.

Stage Three—Structured Interview: A "Structured and Scored Interview" continues to up the odds of a great hire (16%), as well as involving others in the interview process. It contains customized questions that you will ask of every candidate. The questions will be structured to discover fits and mismatches with your top five required traits. (Note: traditional methods of reference checking, unstructured interviews, and resume checking are worth less than 6% in predictability for making a great hire.)

A best practice approach to recruiting will also help to improve retention and productivity of new reps, provided you or your sales manager build a healthy working environment.

▼ ▼ ▼

Take Solomon's advice. Point your arrows at sales candidates who will sell your services and products in the time frame you need them sold. Look for socially-driven and goal-oriented salespeople who show high levels of self-confidence when in front of you. Challenge them with a smile. They will handle this well.

Memorize the character traits, competencies, and personality traits shown above. Pull back the string of a well-tuned bow, and shoot your arrows in an appropriate direction, one that will help you keep from hiring a "fool or any passer-by."

Chapter 23

KNOWING PEOPLE AND THEIR MOTIVATORS

As I've said before, I love to study great coaches and great leaders. During my research, I've watched videos, read articles and books about their lives, philosophies, and systems.

As I looked over various notes and memos and began to separate them, I found many exciting skills for excellence in coaching and its application to sales. Some of these I had already been applying to sales training and to my own sales management work for years. For the first time, I could see the logic in a system that all coaches applied without even understanding the universality in their efforts.

KNOWING PEOPLE

Without a parenting, coaching, or teaching background, you can be at a disadvantage when coaching or managing people. You will have to learn that management approaches must be adjusted to individual preferences for learning, understanding, and gaining their respect. Paying attention to the needs of a child helps a parent understand that effective discipline takes various forms. Teaching a classroom of children with concern for each child causes the teacher to gain a greater appreciation for various types of emotional baggage that impede learning. Guiding young men or women to hit off of a batting tee teaches the baseball or softball instructor the importance of varying the amount of praise given for each hitter. Knowing people turns out to be a prime area of advantage for great teaching, coaching, and parenting.

coach

Each person in the group, team, or family exists as an individual—a one-of-a-kind complex human being with a variety of differences. One of these differences is motivating influence. What does not affect one motivates another toward goal achievement.

As individuals, we approach life from a set of values and beliefs formed by associations and experiences since birth. Whether each person realizes it or not, we behave as a reaction to what is thought to be possible or impossible, right or wrong, real or unreal, proven or unproven, safe or unsafe, good or bad. We grow up with different role models and life events. These affect what we value today: our goal drive, social skills, self-confidence, teamwork, etc.

Today, we have four generations in the workforce: Mature, Boomers, Gen-Xers, and Generation Yers. These waves of new lives born in certain date ranges have different motivations and they do better and produce more within certain environments. Do you work to make the environment an inspirational place for all those who work there?

STARTS WITH THE COACH

Do you understand yourself? Are you more of a social or reserved person? Do you like to respond to things quickly or take a methodical approach to them without being hurried? Do you like to analyze data or work to improve the overall brand and vision of the company? Do you like to serve customers or do you like to work with numbers and process improvements?

> Coach people in the way they want to be coached. To do that well, understand your tendencies and avoid them if a person needs a different style of coaching.

When you learn, do you like to see, feel, or hear the instruction? Which ways help you learn in the best way? Are you motivated by a sense of duty or competition or neither? Do you coach people in the way they want to be coached or do you coach them in the way you want to be coached?

Coach people in the way they want to be coached. To do that well, understand your tendencies and avoid them if a person

211

needs a different style of coaching. Some people like to be given a step-by-step process—others just want you to point them. Certain social types need you to chat with them, encourage them, and recognize them.

As managers who coach, we are each different as well. If we do not realize our own uniqueness, it makes coaching others more complex. We end up not knowing what to adjust in ourselves to make the coaching experience productive for those we coach. We end up coaching others in a manner in which we want to be coached. As a result, our coaching effectiveness decreases.

COACHING VS. SELLING

The golden (ruby or diamond) rule for selling is: "Sell in 'the way' a person wants to be sold!" (see Dr. Tony Alessandra and his work here **www.platinumrule.com**) If a person needs to chat before getting down to business, let them. If someone wants to challenge you, respect their testing of you and respond with confidence and in bullet points. And, if someone is cautious and wants to explore alternatives and their reasoning, provide the data, facts, and time they need to make a decision and do not push them.

> The golden (ruby or diamond) rule for selling is: "Sell in 'the way' a person wants to be sold!".

We also understand this as a parenting rule with our kids as one responds better than another to a particular communication, discipline, or approach. This seems intuitive for us as parents because each of those small ones has individual expressions and preferred methods of learning, thinking, and valuing life. Is it really intuitive? Hmm. I don't think so. Most of the sales managers I know operate as if people were the same. Only the great ones seek to understand the preferred motivating influences for the people they coach.

FOUNDATION INTERVIEW

Since knowing people provides valuable coaching information, I developed a coaching interview to be completed at the beginning of a person's employment as a salesperson. The purpose of this tool is to help you clearly understand the number one motivator of each salesperson on your team. You ask questions, listen, and learn about the needs and problems of a person related to their performance. This helps you get a better feel for the type of coaching that will be most effective. That's why I call it a Foundation Interview. One builds a strong base of knowledge with which to make the environment excellent for a rep's productivity. Interestingly, sales leaders who have done this interview with existing reps have seen an immediate improvement in performance. There are two reasons why: (1) reps were paid attention to, and (2) they thought their employer cared about them. They then reciprocated with increased personal responsibility, belief in themselves, and a better work focus that increased sales.

Here are a few important questions from the interview. You can find additional information about sales coaching at **salesmanage. com/blog or coachsalespeople.com** (where you can download this tool).

- How would you describe your most important accomplishment to date? Why do you choose that one? How does that affect your life today?
- What is the single issue that is keeping you from achieving your maximum potential? What are you doing or plan to do to develop past this? How will this development benefit you?
- What are the three most important things that motivate you in life in order of priority? Why is that one #1 and how does it impact you? Are these also the three most important ones that motivate your sales performance?
- Where do you keep your goals written down? What is your sales and income goal? Why are these important to you? What activity targets do you have each month to reach those?
- Who has had the most impact on your life to-date? Please explain how. How could you impact someone in a similar manner?
- When selling and with a prospect, what is a salesperson's most important skill? Why? How does this help?
- What attributes of a salesperson provide long-term sales success?
- How do you track the progress of your sales goal achievement?
- What issues or problems keep you from performing your best?
- What would you list as the three most important attributes of a sales manager (leader)?
- What would be the three attributes in a sales manager that would hinder you most? Why? What could I do to help you attain your goals?

Remember these important rules. Do not evaluate, offer suggestions for improvement, or do anything to manage the person

in this meeting. Only seek to understand them in order to be a more effective coach for them.

Tell them the purpose of the interview. It's very important that they know the purpose of this session. Let them know that you have a set of questions to ask and that their answers will help you be a better coach for them. You want to help them reach their goals. Explaining this at the beginning shows respect for the person's time, and it shows consideration for their questions about why you want to interview them. It helps to dispel any fear or negative thoughts about being asked to sit down with you as you ask questions.

> *Do not evaluate, offer suggestions for improvement, or do anything to manage the person in this meeting. Only seek to understand them in order to be a more effective coach for them.*

COACHING INFORMATION SHEET

I began to realize while coaching baseball players and salespeople that I needed a single coaching sheet that contained coaching information and goals for each person. Later, as I watched great coaches, many of them kept similar statistics and folders on their players. So, I designed a single page coaching information sheet to include what I learned about them in the coaching interview (see above), performance goals and results, personality traits, personal likes and dislikes, hobbies, spouse's name, and motivational influences. I suggest you do this as well and the discipline of gathering and focusing on this information will make you a better coach—one interested in the progress of the rep. You can get a sample on **coachsalespeople.com**.

▼ ▼ ▼

Great sales managers like you understand that the first stage in an effective coaching system is Knowing People. You get to know your salespeople as individuals with different learning styles and motivational centers.

As you study human nature, you realize that salespeople respond to individualized approaches just like athletes (just like kids). Some like a process—some do not. One needs this and the other needs that. Their motivation may be centered in competition, family, duty, recognition, achievement, or security. Money may not motivate them but they may be motivated by what money provides.

> *Great sales managers like you understand that the first stage in an effective coaching system is Knowing People. You get to know your salespeople as individuals with different learning styles and motivational centers.*

Do a foundation interview with your sales rep(s). Use a set of questions designed to understand each person's motivational needs (#1 motivator), goals, skills, weaknesses, and expectations of you as the sales manager. Doing this will not lessen your effectiveness as their leader. It will strengthen it. The best leaders are the ones with a great desire for results balanced with an understanding that they serve the reps in helping them remove personal and organizational roadblocks in front of their goal achievement.

Go with your salespeople on calls. Get involved in their sales planning. Observe their performance in front of prospects. Do after-the-call coaching. Learn to ask great questions that cause the sales rep to see and act on necessary changes. Get them to see what's happening by saying what they see, and then get them to say what they need to do (see—say—do) Help them do these new skills until they are habits by only working on one or two skill areas at a time. Realize it takes time to build habits. Keep visual sales boards showing activity management and sales progress. Praise specific improvements.

From your interview(s) and observations, develop a coaching and training plan that will improve ramp-up to minimum performance standards. Know your people, their needs, and motivators and it will pay off for them and for you.

Coach Krzyzewski, with four national championships, wants us to remember, "A common mistake among those of us who work in sports (think sales) is spending a disproportional amount of time on "Xs and Os" as compared to time spent learning about people." Know your people as individuals.

Chapter 24

CONNECTING DESIRES TO SALES GOALS

What if I made this statement? **"Most salespeople do not have goals anymore. As a matter of fact, most people I know do not have goals anymore."** I'm not referring to the fun New Year's resolutions that have as much resolve as a cat lying by a warm fireplace in the winter. No, I'm talking about goals you must attain with great effort and discipline—ones for which you track progress without someone asking you to do so—when you are intentional and connected by an emotion that energizes your desire to achieve an objective.

The story of lost specificity and strong responsibilities started years ago for all of us. Let me explain. No matter our culture or nationality, past generations affected the way we behave today. As people struggled for food and shelter or fought against an invader, they developed beliefs and attitudes that formed character strengths like faith, perseverance, and work ethic. Grandparents, mothers, and fathers living in tough times developed these traits and passed them along to their children.

When America was a frontier, people survived by working to stay alive. From before the sun's rise to late at night, people completed tasks in some way connected with finding food, preparing food, or building and maintaining shelter. Life was hard yet simplistic in its requirements for survival. An individual in these times worked to get things done by a certain time of the year. Chop wood, carry water. Hunt food and prepare it. Work the ground and harvest the crops. If you did not work to complete tasks and get things done by a deadline, your life and the lives of your family were in jeopardy.

What happened in the USA? The world changed with events like: the industrial revolution, World War II, Vietnam and baby boomers, economic prosperity, entitlement, welfare, family breakdown, lowered standards, latchkey kids, one-parent families. The family farm disappeared. Cities grew. Life began and ended in a manufacturing plant. Corporations expanded. Living became easy yet emotionally difficult. Fathers left. Mentoring disappeared. And along the way, we as a culture forgot what we believed about what was right and worth the sacrifice.

Two hundred years ago, you could see the forces against you. It was hunger, weather, or an enemy. People who fought well would work, work, work. Eat, sleep, work. Get food, eat, sleep, work. Fight. Love. Protect. A family stayed together when life was difficult.

Romance was not confused with easy sex. Life was an adventure. There were battles to fight and people to love and rescue. Loyalty was a virtue and freedom was won by disciplined individuals. While no generation was perfect, some were stronger than others and children labored with parents to meet the challenges faced by all. The greatest generations were made of tough-minded people who did not pamper their sons and daughters. Instead, by their example, they taught them to love with sacrifice and not to give up when the way was clear yet filled with struggle and loss.

Today, where is the enemy? It's in over-sleeping, over-indulging, over-used credit cards, no savings, student loans, free education, the lottery, anxiety, depression, hopelessness, drugs, multiple choices, broken homes, late maturity, easy life, easy money and a lack of firmly formed values.

Personal responsibility is missing and until someone or something makes the effects and consequences clear, a person languishes in a primordial soup saying, "Woe is me! Life is killing me and thee!"

DESIRE

Two thousand years ago, Jesus Christ, asked a blind man a simple question, "What do you want me to do for you?" While an uncomplicated inquiry, at the center of a true answer lies human passion and need. Today our first response to such a question might be a boat or a trip to Europe or happiness or a million dollars. But, when these are swept away with a smile and the question asked again, the answers of honest people find deeper water. Our true hearts' desires are more along the lines of, "That I have what it takes," "That my children are educated," "My bride feels secure," "My parents are taken care of," "I attain financial peace," "I'm recognized as giving my best," "I am valued for my contribution," "Someone believes I can achieve the goal," "If I work hard it will pay off."

"What do you want?" Give sincere thought to this question, and look for an emotional center behind your focus. Then, in your answer, you may hear a motivation from your heart and deeper still, a connection between commitments, responsibilities, and desire.

Now, sit still and really ask yourself this question:

What do you want?

Today, our society connects itself to another root desire, a self-serving one of fun and pleasure. Too much of it smothers the character strength we need for the challenges we face.

You might ask, "How?" And then say, "I thought hard work produces a reward of fun and pleasure!"

If you live for or enjoy fun and pleasure at the wrong time, they hinder the developing character traits required for a better life—discipline, courage, sacrifice, faith, and perseverance. Fun and pleasure as the center of life blind you to the time that slips by unannounced in the games and television and movies and sports and restaurants. Now, none of these things are bad in themselves. To enjoy them is a by-product of hard work and sacrifice. They only hinder us when they smother the time available for work responsibilities and the effort required for reaching income goals or improving relationships and completing work objectives.

There's another thing that affects our achievement drive—how we talk. When we talk about ourselves, or the things around us in a negative way, desire decreases. Watch what you say about the competition or what you say about your church, your government, your sports team, and the leaders around you. When you see that most of your discussions center around criticism, notice how your desire drops for improving or achieving goals in the areas on which you expend this energy. To increase desire, start seeing and discussing things that show progress. Look for the good in them. Lead yourself and others with words of hope that envision the future. Talk to yourself about what you will do next that will make a difference. Celebrate progress. Realize nothing is perfect. Get others involved in positive declarations and actions. Avoid the negative talk. It doesn't produce anything noble or of lasting value.

Leave the "ought or need or should have" complex behind. "We ought to do this. We need to do this. We should have done this." What I want to know is what are you going to do and when are you going to do it? How are you going to change things? What is your team going to do next to make a difference? Those are the questions that matter. Pave the future with the answers. Act on the desire to achieve.

THE CONNECTION

How do you make a personal connection with a goal? How do you help someone link goal achievement to a desire—one that's important to the heart? How do you do it?

How do you help them do it?

What do I mean when I say "personal connection to a goal?" I mean for you to engage yourself in the fight and the mission. The word "engage" is derived from a French word meaning *to be meshed in the effort or tied up in it; being inextricably entangled and a part of IT.* When I watch the movie *Patriot,* I think of the American Revolution and those men and women involved in the cause of freedom. That is an example of emotional connection and it displays a motivation from the heart that was not quenched by setback. When you are meshed in a quest for something, character strengths emerge in the struggle. Connection to a goal is like the cause of freedom. It may be logical and reasonable, but it is also emotional. When you want the goal at a deep and personal level it keeps your attention even through difficult struggles.

I think this is easier for a business owner than it is for a hired salesperson. Entrepreneurs have a vested interest in goal achievement. They need cash flow. The checkbook is empty. They have to meet payroll next Monday. Vendors want their money. Like 200 years ago, the enemy is easier to see. Work, work, work, fight, and look again at the bank account.

For a hired person, especially someone single with little cash needs or someone with a spouse and a second income, motivation can be less clear. That's because it is not tied into obligations toward others. If high performers do not have a service focus, their motivation usually comes from recognition, fun, pleasure, or competition.

When past experience and prior role models tell us we are perfect or great without pointing to work and effort and persistence, we begin to believe life and achievement should come easy—that everyone should receive a trophy regardless of performance—or that problems should solve themselves in a short amount of time. With this belief we see a lower developed strength of character. The rep lacks perseverance during adversity. If there are multiple opportunities around, salespeople make excuses or scurry over to the competitor or to another job and start over if goal achievement gets tough. Or, they just quit. That's why recruiting character is more important than skills or personality.

Finally, I don't think we have the power to motivate someone. However, we can apply skills to build an inspiring environment for someone who wants to do well and wants to hear the coaching provided. We can ask questions and give advice and training and accountability as they decide to motivate themselves. We do our best at coaching and then remember it's always up to them. Within 30-90 days, we will know if someone has what it takes to contribute at minimum standards.

MAKING THE CONNECTION—YOU

When you frame in a goal, do it with emotion and logic. Realize how you feel now and what you want to feel like in the future. Understand the impact of your goal on your life and on the lives of those you love.

Instead of masking and skirting around the pain, ban denial from your life. Be honest about where you are at home, in your business, and in sales. In other words, do not dive into fun or pleasure or work or anything else to avoid the thinking required for understanding the reality of your situation and its impact now and in the future. Know where you stand and where you want to go by when.

Next, get advice, get training, get a new education. Get around people who can help you. Find people to associate with who want to grow themselves and are meshed in their own goal achievement. They do not have to be in your industry. Ask for their help.

Go further. Whether you own a business or you operate alone as a salesperson, create a board, a group of people you respect, to whom you present your current situation and future plans. Get their counsel and reaction. Listen. Put aside your ego. Report back to them with a specific checklist of goals with important tasks and projects to complete. Report to them each quarter. Be accountable to them.

Regarding sales, and as a high-activity sales professional, do the work at the beginning of the book and decide your income goal. Then, using the instruction in this book translate that income goal into a sales goal with its critical selling activity targets. Focus on ob-

226

taining results from these activities. Keep track. Measure progress. Manage your activity. Do the Right Levels of Right Activities™.

MAKING THE CONNECTION—OTHERS

As a business owner, entrepreneur, or sales leader, few high-activity salespeople you hire have their #1 motivation centered on duty and reaching your sales budgets. They find motivation in other places: in their own desires for security, recognition, competition, or achievement (often defined by money earned).

Find the number one motivation for each sales rep. Most of the time you can tie this desire to an income goal or sales goal or both. In most instances, the motivational needs of a salesperson can be connected with a sales goal. If you have recruited the right people, the sales goal that they require for income needs will be above your minimum performance standard.

To help you and them, have your salespeople complete the survival numbers exercise described at the beginning of the book (download a free tool for this at **coachsalespeople.com**). When your reps or rep complete this simple goal-setting exercise, they will know what amount of money it takes just for them to survive. They will also know their "Better Lifestyle" numbers—the amount of money they want for savings, children's education, new car, better home, etc. This exercise may or may not trigger a heart-felt motivation. Recognition or being number one, for example, has nothing to do with money. Know your people well. Understand their base motivational needs.

A sales board developed around the number one motivator of each rep will provide greater inspiration than a company's budget target. To coach beyond quota, stay away from a budget focus. Place measurements and encouragement on motivators that inspire.

BREAKTHROUGH

David Johnson, Eric's sales manager, watched Eric walk into his office and sit down. David saw that he was carrying the pre-work assigned prior to their meeting. He was relieved to see Eric because he had wanted an opportunity to help him for several months now.

In the last three years, David had enjoyed Eric in his role selling for the company. He had watched Eric take off with natural talent only to plateau in a flurry of mismanaged time, priorities, and habits. When David had tried to approach Eric regarding his time, he had received smiles and assurances, but no changes. The timing had never been right for Eric to really want to hear instruction designed to help him get better.

For the next two hours, David asked questions and listened and learned about Eric's wife, her pregnancy and her desire to stop working and take care of their children. He asked Eric about the frustrations he was experiencing and watched his face change as he grew emotional regarding his wife's condition and his need to make more money. Eric mentioned Jessica and the success she was enjoying and the system she talked about using. When David asked him if he wanted his help, Eric said, "Yes, things HAVE to change. Will you teach me the same system you've taught Jessica?"

David asked Eric to pull out his pre-work, a sheet of numbers. Some of the figures were budgeted survival numbers for Eric and his wife. The rest were related to their lifestyle needs: general savings, college savings for their children, debt reduction, and house improvements. The final monthly income amount reflected these and all their financial needs including future ones. It was $7,500 per month.

At the bottom of the sheet, Eric had written and averaged his last six months of income from commissions. His take home pay had been $5,300 per month. As they both looked at the difference, David asked, "What do you think?" Eric replied, "I'm working so hard now, I don't know where I'm going to find the time to sell this much more—it's about a 30% increase!" What David said next helped to calm Eric and would be something he would hold onto in the weeks to come. "Don't think about the goal, focus on the weekly activity levels. Now, let's see what they will be."

However, without an activity history of prospects, appointments, and quotes, they could not figure out the monthly levels necessary to achieve a $7,500 income. So, he and David began to make conservative assumptions for the important ratios. They arrived at the following:

To earn $7,500, would require Eric to make monthly sales of $50,000.
An average size sale for Eric had been $7,800.
Which meant that he would need to make 6.4 sales per month.
With a 33% close ratio, he would have to get out 19.25 quotes.
With a 90% opportunity ratio, he would need to do 21.3 first appointments.

David asked Eric what he saw. Eric replied, "1 appointment per day and I'm there! I never thought about focusing on activity and seeing the weekly activity required." He paused for a moment, turned to David, and said, "I can do this. It's only 1 new appointment a day."

And, he did. As a matter of fact, he increased his earning to over $8,500 per month by learning to change his lead generation methods to ones that produced prospects considering higher dollar investments. He pushed paperwork to non-primetime selling hours. Eric also adjusted his appointment setting by geographical area, eliminating unnecessary travel time. He listened carefully to David, talked with Jessica, and learned a great amount in the newly designed sales meetings.

When he attended sales meetings, he found that David focused them on the activity management process, and as he looked at his numbers and listened to the other reps, he learned better ideas about appointment setting strategies and getting referrals. Eric's hard work ethic became channeled into more effective and efficient methods for using time and getting critical sales activities up to planned levels. Sales at higher levels were a result of this focus.

Three months later, Eric's wife came home to prepare the house for a new arrival. As Eric's income increased, they began to put money aside for the family's future needs.

Now, let's look at the agendas for the high-performance meetings that David attended.

Chapter 25

LEADING HIGH-ACTIVITY SALES MEETINGS

Meetings occur everyday in several different venues. A family talks about an upcoming vacation. Two people talk about current movies. Lovers stroll in Central Park and talk. A man and his sons sit in a boat and just fish.

Everywhere you look meetings happen. While the examples above are from everyday life, the ones that matter to sales production must engage us in a way that help us achieve our income needs.

Have you attended meetings without agendas that were boring and that got off topic? After you left, how did you feel? The meetings we hold or participate in are not always productive. Years ago, after researching the profit losses due to ineffective meetings, the Xerox

Corporation spent several million dollars to improve them. They found it was that important.

Lead sales meetings that support your people and their sales goal achievement. Hold these once per week for one hour or less. Their purpose will be to help sales reps clearly understand weekly activity, personal and team goal achievement progress, and to cause the reps to remain focused on the most important activities. Below I have listed the objectives, agenda, rules, and standards of a high-performance sales meeting. I hope these ideas help you improve the quality and effectiveness of your sales meetings.

SALES MEETING OBJECTIVES

* To bring celebration into sales work
* To remain accountable to weekly activity rates
* To make adjustments to plan
* To report progress of sales performance projects
* To sharpen a selling skill or improve attitudes

Prior to the sales meeting, have the sales reps update the sales board. If you use **SalesActivities.com**, it will automatically produce this board from prospects entered, first appointments set and held, quotes presented, and sales made for the month-to-date. Otherwise, do this with an Excel or Google spreadsheet.

SALES MEETING AGENDA

1. Start by asking for any celebrations from the past week.
2. Show the sales board and look at month-to-date sales progress.
   - Ask for any observations on the numbers.
   - Point out those reps with good activity numbers or those on goal.
3. Find specific actions to applaud or progress to praise. Perhaps, mention something you observed in a rep during the week.
4. Give each rep 2-3 minutes to talk about
   - Last week activities, progress, and what they learned.
   - Sales-in-progress (size and dollars)
   - Upcoming activities and their focus for next week.
5. Report on any sales team performance projects.
6. End with a short learning session or inspirational thought.

SALES MEETING RULES/STANDARDS

1. Do not berate, criticize, or call out a rep's bad performance.
2. Start and end the meeting on time.
3. Focus on ending the meeting on a challenging, inspirational, or upbeat note.

Hold one-on-one meetings with salespeople who show signs of getting behind. Manage their progress. Coach their improvement. Stay focused on helping them reach their income goals in a way that satisfies their motivational needs. Make sure they know that you believe they have what it takes.

High-activity sales meetings are critical to the performance and spirit of a team.

Hold them every week. You can do this. Do this.

Chapter 26

COACHING RESULTS FROM ACTIVITY MANAGEMENT

I have worked as an entrepreneur and business owner for around 30 years. During that time, if I sold something we ate well and if I did not sell something we did not eat well. If sales occurred the lights stayed on and if sales did not happen the lights went off. I worked on 100% commission. After one sale occurred, I had to find another and another and another for 30 years.

Do you relate to this—the ups and downs and the uncertainty of not knowing if the mortgage will be paid at the end of the month? My bride worked inside the home. We had three young boys running around the house. I left each morning to cold call sales managers. I prospected for someone who would give me an appointment, someone who thought I might be of value. At the same time, bills were due, food kept disappearing, and my friendly utility company thought I should pay them each month.

RESULTS

While success is not about results, we do have commitments and responsibilities toward objectives that affect others. As a high-activity, sales professional, I experience this reality as I watch cash flow and the needs of my family and my company. Life is full of consequences. If I go fishing every day then I will experience an outcome. If I leave my grass for weeks, this will cause a forest to grow up and into my house. If. If. If. ...

I was in Ohio working for Goodyear Tire and Rubber and a group of men asked me to play in their annual Hearts tournament. Now, you may not be familiar with this popular card game. Played in groups of four, a person attempts to keep from winning the Queen of Spades (worth 13 points) and any hearts (1 point each) during the 13 rounds of cards played. The object is to have the lowest number of points during each round. However, if you happen to take them all during a single hand, the Queen and the hearts, then you "run the table" and give everyone else 26 points. That evening with one particular grouping of cards dealt to me, I attempted to "run the table" and after taking the Queen of Spades and 12 hearts, I lost the last heart to someone else, and instead of giving everyone else 26 points, I received 25 points. At that moment I exclaimed, "If only ...," and proceeded to explain how I was just one point shy of a run. There were other times that evening that I made a similar statement, "If only ..." At the end of the evening, I was awarded the annual "If only" trophy.

Let me tell you, it's all about giving our best to meet the obligations we accept. It's not about "if only." All the exclamations and "if only" statements will not make a difference in the income you receive and the deposit you make at the bank. Be smart. Get better. Focus on the activity that leads to results. Talk about what you will do differently- the actions that will lead to better results. Then, do these actions for the benefit of others and as a personal responsibility, or do them for recognition, security, or to achieve, but do them. Work to obtain a satisfactory or favorable outcome as you do the right levels of the right activities with the right people. This occurs when you close the sales that are pending and, with a steady stream of self-generated leads, first appointments, and quotes presented, achieve the amount of sales you need for a specific income and lifestyle.

ACTIVITY LEADS TO RESULTS

Many sales managers pound on their reps for results. They keep them fearful and focused on their lack of sales. They do not teach them how to manage their activities, so no one gets smarter and a great number of reps change employment. These managers experience excessive turnover and it costs their company thousands of dollars to recruit and lose each rep.

Entrepreneurs or lone sales professionals often behave the same way. They beat themselves up for poor sales results and they keep a laser focus on one number—the sales closed number. This leads to a fearful and anxious existence. It's similar to coaching a little league baseball team and allowing the fathers to berate their sons about their batting averages. I've seen fathers kill their kids' batting averages and I've seen sales professionals do the same thing with their sales numbers. Both forget about practice and about the process. **Smart activity leads to the results you want.** While you focus on doing the right activities, you watch for progress toward the results you need. Take a tip from legendary Coach John Wooden, who said, "Never mistake activity for achievement." Remember that winning comes from doing your best at the steps that lead to excellence. Make yourself better today and watch for evidence that this improvement is enough to achieve your goals.

ACTIVITY MANAGEMENT

I wrote this book to help you manage the right levels of the right sales activities™ to reach your income goals. The online application, **SalesActivities.com**, was designed for the same reason. Whether you use it, a yellow pad, or a spreadsheet, I want you to keep track of your sales process, its activity levels, and the results it produces. Then, you can work to make things better.

Great sports coaches and sales coaches know that there is a process involved in achieving excellence. Many football lovers regard Vince Lombardi as the greatest coach of all time. Winning five NFL championships and two Super Bowl championships, he declared, "Every game boils down to doing the things you do best and doing them over and over again." High-activity sales professionals prospect, set and hold first appointments, make presentations, and get out quotes. They do these over and over and over again. They do enough of these key activities to win, to achieve the results important for their motivations and duties.

In the absence of a process, a sales manager pounds on another human being, the salesperson, for results. Try pounding on yourself for results. Try pounding on your son for good grades. Try pounding on your wife or husband for a better marriage. Yes, just try it. Maybe you have. I can tell you from both experience and observation, it won't work. It will kill the spirit or inspire rebellion. If you get overly focused on results, you will forget about the process, the work, and the love that precedes the results you want. Quality activities lead to quality results. Poor or low activity leads to losses, an inferior product, and bad relationships.

Results come from the activities that precede them, from the number of them and the quality of them. With a process, a salesperson and a sales leader can look at areas for improvement. Coaching can occur. Together, they can look upstream at lead generation, or appointment setting, or any of the steps in the process and work to improve those that need correction. That attention to disciplined change makes the steps of a process important to both the teacher and the student. Through targeted practice and instruction, it gives both the ability to make results downstream of precipitating actions line up with necessary goals.

IMPORTANT RATIOS

As you work to help someone manage their actions, remember to keep track of the various activity ratios of high-activity sales professionals: opportunity ratio, closing ratio, and referral ratio. Each of these tells us about areas of improvement for managing our way to results.

For example, a salesperson generates leads but does not set enough first appointments. In this case, the opportunity to make a presentation and give someone a quote diminishes. The training focus could be on generating leads that meet the ideal prospect profile, or the salesperson could work on appointment setting skills. In another coaching direction, what if a salesperson sets appointments but not enough quotes occur? Then, a look at the face-to-face sales process could uncover poor rapport building or an inability to ask the right need-development questions.

Hope increases when a plan emerges. Pounding on yourself or others for results changes hope to discouragement. Do not do this. Do your best to work a plan of improvement through activity management. Analyze the reason for a lack of results. Set your mind on changing your sales numbers by increasing activity levels or changing the activity quality. You can do this. Do it for yourself. Do it for those you coach. Do it.

COACHING

You know now that results depend on activities. You can teach others that **the *Right Levels of the Right Activities*™ held with the right people lead to sales goal achievement.** Help yourself and others improve sales results from activity management.

Discipline yourself to use an activity management system where you can record your numbers. Focus on the process. Set goals for activity levels. Hold weekly sales meetings. Put a sales board on the wall. Make that sales board contain columns from left to right showing the activities leading to results. Keep it simple. It is simple. The work to get better is hard. Do it.

Manage critical selling activities. Analyze your numbers. Understand the relationship between opportunity ratios (first appointments to quotes) and closing ratios (quotes to sales). Work to make these ratios better. Know yours and know those of your sales team so that you can help everyone manage the right amounts of activities. As you get better, you will recognize and set minimum activity standards. You will know what is minimum, average, and great relevant to the right amount of critical activity levels.

When someone joins your team, two things will happen. One, you will know what activity levels lead to what goals. Two, they will step into a team where the culture recognizes and embraces activity management for the right reasons—to help people fulfill their motivating needs and create the lifestyle they envision. You will make the atmosphere one of specificity, encouragement, and greatness.

Chapter 27

HIGHLY-SPIRITED TEAMS WITH HOPE AND COMMITMENT

When I was 12, I was fortunate to play third base for a Little League team that won the city championship. Before each game, you could hear and see the spirit of our team. Imagine a bunch of 10-12 year olds hanging on a dugout fence singing a ballad about "Ole Uncle Mort he sawed off his shorts, he measured bout four foot two ..." At the top of our voices and with our still forming lungs, our song filled the baseball park. Parents of the opposing team stopped and watched. Those in the refreshment stands smiled and gazed in our direction. Across the diamond, our opponents looked on with amazement and I believe respect, perhaps even fear. As I look back, I realize that many of our games were won before they began.

Years later, when my son reached the same age, we relived my youth in a group of Little Leaguers that ending their season with a record of 17-2. Instead of singing before each game, we worked through drills as a team, each cheering for the other, balls flying around in an orchestrated pattern, a well-honed choreography. As the game approached, we ran around the field as a unit—no one player out running the other. Midway through the season, parents of an opposing team commented about how difficult it was to beat a team that knew each other so very well and seemed to have so much fun.

In both instances, do you know who fabricated those wonderful environments? The coaches. And, the power of it swept through the teams and into their bats and hearts. I was lucky to remember and appreciate the coaches in my youth and the character strength they built in each of us through hard work, encouragement, and a simple urging to give our best on the field.

▼ ▼ ▼

Great coaches develop a winning spirit of goal achievement among uniquely different human beings. Whether their teams are behind or ahead, competitively outclassed or leading the field, these coaches continually build commitment, hope, and passion into people.

Some coaches coach well but do not recruit talent well. As a result, their teams do not contain clones of perfectly birthed performers. Instead, they contain people with ordinary skills who achieve goals beyond their abilities.

Other coaches, perhaps recognizing their own coaching limitations, recruit well. They then manage talented people into winning teams.

Whether coaches recruit well, or coach well, great coaches create a winning spirit through an environment in which individuals thrive and accomplish their best work!

These coaches do not motivate people. Instead, they create motivating environments in which people want to grow, in which they want to work together, in which they have common goals. Each person accomplishes more on the team than they do alone.

> *Great coaches develop a winning spirit of goal achievement among uniquely different human beings. Whether their teams are behind or ahead, competitively outclassed or leading the field, these coaches continually build commitment, hope, and passion into people.*

Coaching greats infuse a spiritual vitality into work—a winning way wrapped around three main areas of focus—commitment, hope, and passion.

COMMITMENT

This is where it begins. With goals. With the end point in mind. With clear job descriptions. With a push the boat off from shore, do not look back decision about what a coach stands for, about what he or she wants the team to stand for. Standards are clear. The direction is certain.

In Lewis Carroll's book, *Alice in Wonderland*, a great coaching moment occurs between Alice and the Cat.

> Alice: Would you tell me, please, which way I ought to go from here?
> The Cat: That depends a good deal on where you want to get to.

Alice: I don't much care where.

The Cat: Then it doesn't much matter which way you go.

Alice: ... so long as I get somewhere.

The Cat: Oh, you're sure to do that, if only you walk long enough.

Alice didn't care about results or a commitment to the future. She just wanted to "get somewhere." Do you want to get to a specific performance and income level, or do you just want to work hard? Which is it? In others words, "What level of performance or income is important?" Write it down. Having commitments means being specific about responsibilities. The great motivating speaker, Zig Ziglar, once commented, "Many people are wandering generalities instead of meaningful specifics." Both The Cat and Zig tell us to stop wandering around and pick somewhere to go.

On a great sales team, new hires can smell the certainty of direction: the clear, un-confusing signals, the here's what we're about purpose of our organization. This brings them into a place of inspiration and gives them a destination for their hope. For, even in the dark places of caves and wells, everyone looks for the light and wants out of the darkness and back to where clarity makes opportunities more certain.

On these great teams, the goals are before us and the targets well defined. This means more than a scoreboard, which only tells us where we end up. Yes, for high-activity sales professionals it means working to achieve an income level, a sales goal, a closing percentage, and an opportunity ratio.

Team members know where the coach stands and what is important. The values are clear. Honesty. Hard work. Personal responsibility. Customer satisfaction.

Processes are simple and followed, but are not above being changed. Processes are built to help people achieve commitments, not for the sake of processes.

People speak the truth in one-on-ones and in meetings. They face reality. They understand the consequences and the rewards. They report profit and loss and compare them to their personal or team goals.

And, most importantly, whether the coach has great people skills or not, each person on the team knows their coach is committed to their personal success as well as the team's success. This is never in doubt.

HOPE

Great coaches believe the individual will win and the team will win. What they do and say, when behind or ahead of goal, whether near defeat or after a loss, builds confidence in eventual success. They keep hope alive in those around them.

People are not perfect, but imperfect. They make mistakes. They lose their way. Their leaders guide them back into safe harbors and into the light. Even if they have to help reps find new leadership and new employment, great coaches will do this in a manner that helps them keep their dignity and honor as a person. When reps remain in their care and under their leadership, they show belief in them.

This is not to say that they coach in a King Arthur's Camelot world of unreality. No, great coaches are realists; they have a healthy amount of skepticism. But, if they commit to a rep as a team member, they will always do and say things to help the rep succeed even in the face of great difficulty and slow progress.

When reps remain on the team, they know their coach believes they have what it takes even during mistakes, when behind goal, or after forgotten commitments. They may not enjoy the coaching process during these times. It may not be an experience that feels good. They will know, however, at the end of it, that the coach cared about them and did things to protect their hope while they grew stronger at their responsibilities.

Hopeless teams or individuals seldom pull victory from the jaws of defeat. When hope diminishes, when we stop reaching for life, it ebbs away from us faster than before. As coaches, we have an obligation to create an environment that inspires people and their hope in a future. While none of us are perfect, the best of us, although we may be fighting to believe in the light ahead, still endeavor to keep encouragement at high levels for those we lead.

With this hopeful spirit carried away from the office, salespeople walk through just one more door. They pick the phone up more times per hour. Their voice inflections cast belief into a prospect's wavering decision. They win more often. They keep the faith.

PASSION

How do great coaches go about their work? With passion. With energy. You can look at them and see the working spirit of committed hope. You can see the early morning rise and the late evening commitment when the load is great on everyone.

They do not count the hours at work. Why not? Why don't they count them until forty pass by and the bell rings to go home? Why not stop when the five o'clock rush begins? Why not slip into the crowd with the rest? Nothing wrong with that—right? Wrong. Leaders do not allow a sense of entitlement in a forty-hour week to creep into their soul and wear away the fabric of their character. Sometimes they weather tougher times and longer hours. When those hours are required and sacrifice is necessary for the greater good, real leaders do what it takes to protect their families and those in their care.

Go and find William Danforth's book, *I Dare You!* Originally written in 1936, it is still sold by the American Youth Federation or you can find copies at Amazon. The thirty-seventh edition was printed in 2002. In this wonderful book, Mr. Danforth, then the founder and former Chairman of the Board and President of the Ralston Purina Company, writes to his salespeople about leading executives, "... but I did find one common attribute in every one of them. That is energy. I think if you look at the propelling force of any successful executive, you will find it is energy. True, you may find an occasional person who has succeeded in spite of the lack of energy, but for every one of such you will find twenty or thirty have succeeded because of it."

Yes, great coaches fan the flame of passion in salespeople by their own example. With an intense work ethic, they throw themselves into the tasks and thinking at hand in an effort to win the day. They engage their emotions, thoughts, and actions toward achieving a sales goal. They accept the responsibilities of a sales budget and the care of people needing training, encouragement, and someone to lead the way. They even take on serving in the attainment of another person's needs and wants. They cheer. They challenge and they confront to help out in the battle for results.

When they speak, it may not be with great oration, or with a gift of fine words. But, it is with strength, commitment, and hope. They know what they believe in and they go about work with the passion of a patriot.

Their purpose is clear: Do their very best right now with what they have and for what they believe in. And, they direct this passion to help the team and each individual successfully achieve. Passion, hope and commitment prevail for the benefit of others.

Chapter 28

ACTION STEPS—COACHING AND ACHIEVING SALES GOALS

We are at the end of "Coaching Highly-Spirited Sales Teams into Goal Achievement." Together, we are just beginning a journey of activity management and help for you and your team's sales goal achievement.

In this part, we began our education and leadership development with a focus on a best practice recruiting system designed to find a talented high-activity sales professional. You studied three stages of a recruitment funnel: screening, validated profiles, and structured interviews. These stages work together to increase your chances of finding someone with the right competencies, character, and personality traits.

We then moved our thoughts to coaching. *Knowing People* was introduced as the first stage of great coaching. In this stage, through observation, profiles, and one-on-one interviews, you learned the importance of finding the #1 motivator of each rep. In this stage, you worked to understand a salesperson's unique and common support needs, both personal and business.

Today, fewer people around you understand their own motivations and responsibilities. Get to know your reps as individuals. As you ask questions and listen, you begin to know more about their passions and most important needs. Using this knowledge, you can work to help each rep connect with sales and income goals. As you do so, you will help increase the motivating power within their hearts.

The high-performance sales meetings you lead will bring celebration into sales work. They will help sales reps remain focused on the *Right Levels of the Right Activities.*™ You will use activity management to help coach results—individual and team sales goal achievement.

And, most importantly, just like a great sports coach, you will lead highly spirited teams with a commitment toward goal achievement, a passion for sales, and hope for the future. Whether up or down, behind or ahead, you will manage a team of individuals.

▼ ▼ ▼

GOALS AND DIRECTION

Henry Ford once remarked that, "Obstacles are those frightful things you see when you take your eyes off your goal." I know what he means from experience. Years ago, with the lights about to be cut off in my house, as I was starting a new business, I picked up a phone that seemed to weigh 85 pounds. Somehow I got through those cold calls. It took real faith. I was aware of my goals in vivid technicolor: Keep the lights on. Pay my mortgage. Keep the house. Buy food. The basics.

Today, after 30 years of coaching salespeople and sales leaders, I find a lack of specificity and a loss of direction growing among them. When I take a salesperson through a series of questions during training, it becomes obvious to everyone that the person works without a particular target in mind. Why?

Maybe it's because of not being accountable, responsible, and aware of living above survival needs. What do I mean? Do your reps know how much money it takes to survive, not get ahead and improve their lifestyle, and not to pay for their child's college education, but to survive? I'm asking you if they know the exact number—the **exact** number? Have they added up their basic fiscal needs?

Many salespeople perform around their survival number. Intuitively, because of a need for money at certain times of the month to pay bills, and to keep the household running, they force themselves to pick up their activities, follow up, get quotes out, etc. During each sales period, they feel agony in a yo-yo effect of emotional ups and downs around this minimal performance level.

Yet needs exist beyond what it takes to survive in the present. The future makes its demands upon today and we must recognize them to survive in the future. That's why a savings account is important. Roofs and cars wear out. The unexpected happens. When we do not set aside money, we pay the piper through credit cards.

Finally, do not necessarily accept the corporate, sales, budget number in your planning or coaching. That is, not unless your company sets it above or equal to what will provide enough commissions for your team's income needs. What does a sales budget have to do with the reality of their survival and future lifestyle needs? Remember, the company you work for develops sales budgets and goals based on company needs, not yours or your team's needs. So, set your income goal and corresponding sales goal based on what your team wants to achieve for themselves or their families. If the sales budget is higher, then lift yours and their motivation to that height!

Now, work hard at the high-activity sales process and begin managing its activities for your team's passions and interests and to help your company thrive.

LEADS AND APPOINTMENTS

Opening the gates to lead generation starts the downstream flow of prospects—a stream that you will keep at a steady flow. That means you will attend the necessary number of functions, visit with centers of influence, go to trade show events, and work in other lead channels until you have a list of names to prospect. You will continually feed this list at a rate that you will set; 10, 15, 20 names a month. It's up to you and your sales metrics, your ratios, and your income needs.

Do not prospect a random group of leads. You will run all potential leads through your profile of an ideal prospect. Doing this will help your prospecting efficiency and opportunity ratios. You will work those leads that have the greatest chance in turning into appointments. In appointments with prospects that you qualify ahead of time, you will more often find people who will want a quote to solve needs and problems that you fill and solve. This will help your sales effectiveness increase.

With high-priority leads, you will schedule time each week to call for first appointments. In these prospect meetings, you will ask a standard set of questions for the purpose of discovering if what you sell will help someone. If you believe this is true, you will customize your presentations and quotes to show how your products and services will fill needs, solve problems, or satisfy wants. These presentations may occur on the spot or at a subsequent appointment.

As you work hard, you may find sales work to be difficult—especially if you focus on being responsible for results. Instead work on your character. Make yourself better. Increase your work ethic. Eschew negativity. Change your approach. These things will change you and the results you get. As Seth Godin mentions in his book *Linchpin,* "Become a linchpin in the world and the people around you will tell your story for you."

Build a team of people around you who want to pursue excellence in sales or coaching salespeople. Listen to their counsel. Challenge each other. Read books together. Share stories that increase hope and teach new truths.

Find a cause. Flame your passion for work. Love your products and services. Know what they do in the lives of those you serve. Work on bringing authentic stories and passions for how you help your customers into your presentations. Be a success by giving your best for the benefit of others. Then, communicate these stories on your website, in your social media, and with your prospects.

MANAGING ACTIVITIES

Identify the stages of your sales funnel. Keep them simple. For example, prospects, appointments, sales-in-progress. Focus on managing the Right Levels of the Right Activities.™ Find a minimum number of prospects each month to keep the funnel pressure strong. Then, set and hold the number of appointments necessary to produce the right amount of quotes according to the closing ratio you estimate for yourself. Finding prospects, holding first appointments, and giving closing presentations—these are the critical selling activities. Do them at the right levels and good things will happen.

Do not allow activity levels to fall below your calculated standards. Keep them elevated according to your estimates for opportunity and closing ratios. Later, you can change these as you have a history of truth in recorded activity numbers.

Remember that elephants are eaten one bite at a time. With only thirty-one days in a month, make sure your activity levels remain consistent and steady. How do you do this? With a sales board. Put one up as a visual reminder of your activity targets, or use a spreadsheet, or an online application like **SalesActivities.com** If you need ten prospects, six first appointments, and 3 quotes per week to average 1 sale per week, then make sure you record your actual numbers. All of your favorite sports teams do this to understand their performance. You do it too.

Do not kid yourself by recording activities that are not critical or activities that do not meet the definition of a first appointment or a presentation. This will hurt you and you alone. It will backfire on you as your funnel dries up or it does not produce the amount of revenue that you need to feed yourself, your family, or to keep yourself employed. Tell the truth. Keep an accurate count. Be conservative with your numbers. This will help you and perhaps even surprise you at the end of the sales period with greater than expected income.

Do not allow an "it's all about results" emphasis to keep you from measuring the steps in your sales process. Do keep track of results, and at the same time, if you have a sales team, put a priority on training people to increase activity levels to appropriate levels relative to their personal goal achievement. Also, pay attention to the sales skills development that will make them more effective prospectors and appointment setters. Teach them how to handle the first appointment with professionalism focusing on questions that draw out the wants, needs, and problems of the prospect. Then, coach their presentation skills. If you are by yourself, an entrepreneur, then do these things for yourself. Seek out books, training programs, and mentors to help you understand the nuances of the selling process with its skills, attitudes, and tools. Make yourself better.

Throughout your sales career, work hard to be irreplaceable in the lives of your customers or clients. Build referrals. How? Well, while some will say that's a book in itself, I will give you one attitude and mantra to guide you. Think about and say the word "we." Become a partner with those you sell to by thinking about their business or life and how you can help, as a partnering vendor, in increasing pride, pleasure, peace, or profit. By realizing "it's all about them" and that you are an integral, if sometimes small part of it, this will make all the difference in your sales, marketing, and service. Even if you sell what many think to be a commodity, this "we" focus will make a valuable difference in the minds of the prospects you approach and the customers you serve.

It will make a big difference for those you coach as well.

▼ ▼ ▼

Here you are again. Coaching yourselves and coaching the salespeople who sign on to take this high-activity road with you. As long as they are on the team, you will believe they have what it takes.

▼ ▼ ▼

You will because I believe this for you. I do believe this because you are now, I hope, a part of our team. And, we at SalesManage

Solutions and **SalesActivities.com** thank you for joining our organization of high-activity sales professionals. This book is finished, but our life-long learning process continues. Let's stop spinning our wheels and go reach our goals—lifestyle goals.

Part V

FINAL THOUGHTS
AND TOOLS

Chapter 29

REMEMBER TO ...

MAKE LIFESTYLE GOALS MORE CONCRETE

Over the past 25 years, I've studied common behaviors and attitudes of great salespeople. In a fast sales cycle, from 30 minutes to 90 days, they stay oriented toward their long-term goals while managing their daily activities. During each cycle, they employ a simple system for success, and then they do it again, and again.

The greatest salespeople in the world manage activities with PASS™. Their secret is knowing how to translate their lifestyle goals into daily sales activities.

A direct mathematical relationship exists between sales activities and revenue, and thus between sales activities and lifestyle goals. Developing a formula from the mathematical relationship between activities and results enables you to know how much you need to make to achieve your desired lifestyle.

MAKE THE NUMBERS WORK FOR YOU

Understand YOUR formula. Make conservative estimates for the number of prospects you must find to generate the right number of first appointments, quotes, and SALES. If you want to use our wizard and online application, go to **SalesActivities.com** and get started.

SalesActivities.com calculates your percentage of sales vs. quotes, percentage of sales from referrals, average quote size, and average sales size. Displayed in easy-to-understand charts and percentages, these ratios will clarify how you need to spend your time each day.

Imagine knowing exactly what you need to do to make enough money for the month! You'll know when to focus less on networking events and more on setting up appointments with the prospects you already have. With the time saved on unproductive activities, you can start chipping away at the next month. Our application promotes that kind of efficiency.

Start using hard numbers to guide your activities. What's your "opportunity ratio"? Or, how many appointments produce a quote? Knowing the answers to these questions will tell you when to look for a new market or to better qualify your leads. You'll know when to ask for more referrals or work on your face-to-face closing skills.

LEARN MORE ABOUT THE BOOK

At **SellingBEYONDSurvival.com** you will find more information about the book and my reasons for writing it. I will also place some free training videos, articles, and other free information there to help you continue learning and to improve your activity management.

LEARN MORE ABOUT ACTIVITY MANAGEMENT

We will soon have additional learning packages available for your purchase and use, perhaps by the time you receive this book. You will find more information about the following tools by visiting **SalesActivities.com**.

- Audiobooks
- Online video training packages
- Training manuals for sales teams and managers
- Distributor packages

READ IMPORTANT SALES MANAGEMENT BLOGS AND ARTICLES HERE

SalesActivities.com/blog

DESCRIPTION: (Please subscribe.) *This blog is focused on activity management and how to get better at making sure that you or your reps keep critical sales activities high enough to achieve income goals at necessary lifestyle levels (or beyond budget levels).*

CoachSalespeople.com

DESCRIPTION: *I am writing this blog to complete another book for sales managers and leaders. Here, you will find ideas about culture development and about coaching sales reps. Please sign up if you find this of interest and if you want to learn about leadership and techniques for coaching people to change their habits for the better.*

Salesmanage.com/blog

DESCRIPTION: *This is our company's main blog and website. My business partner, Steve Suggs, author of* Can They Sell, *posts training videos to help sales managers select the best reps.* I also post here primarily about coaching and leadership for sales managers. Please sign up for automatic updates.

LINK UP

Please link up with me. I enjoy chatting and learning with those who have a genuine interest in high-activity sales. The pace is usually fast. The conversations are challenging and fun to join and the insight provided is often invaluable. Here are some places to find me.

linkedin.com/in/lancecooper
twitter.com/LanceACooper
twitter.com/SalesActivities
facebook.com/lance.cooper.568

CONTACT US FOR SPEAKING/TRAINING ENGAGEMENTS

To keep sales managers from hanging themselves with the names of reps on their chests, I design sales coaching and leadership training for companies with approximately 10 or more sales managers. I also design, deliver, facilitate, or conduct train-the-trainers for these same companies.

www.lancecooper.com
www.salesmanage.com/contact
865-675-2002

Chapter 30

SELF OR TEAM MANAGEMENT TOOLS

I love to develop tools. Good ones help us develop in our roles, and they help us do our jobs better. In sales, a self-assessment tool gives us direction for improvement by providing a focus on areas that impact consistent performance and goal-achievement.

After we look at our attitudes and competencies with a self-assessment, we can construct additional tools to:

- Determine necessary income levels for both survival and lifestyle needs
- Convert survival/lifestyle incomes into sales goals
- Convert sales goals into the "Right Levels of Right Activities™"
- Track actual vs. target activity levels (prospects, appointments, and quotes)

- Calculate important efficiency levels with opportunity and closing ratios
- Calculate the average actual vs. target quote and sales levels
- Track percentage of sales from referred leads
- Track actual vs. target sales and income levels

In this final part of the book, I will provide two management tools to help you begin or improve your journey as a high-activity sales professional—(1) *Activity Management Self-Assessment,* and (2) *Survival and Lifestyle Goal Setting.* Additional tools and resources will be provided at the online locations shown in the previous section.

Activity Management Self-Assessment (directions)

There are twenty-four (24) statements that explain an attitude, competency, knowledge or skill related to effective activity management. Please read them and mark the level (1 = never, 7 = all the time) that describes your strength proficiency for each.

After looking at your lowest areas, write down actions that you believe will help you improve your activity management. Over the next few weeks, begin these strategic actions and stick with them until you see progress. Also, look for additional sources of learning that help to reinforce your development. Here are five examples of actions you might right down.

- Keep a prospect list and add 10 new prospects to it each week.
- Schedule weekly, appointment phoning time on my calendar.
- Track my actual vs. target levels of first appointments set and held.

- Track my actual vs. target quoting levels.
- Do a forecast, at least weekly, of my end-of-the month sales.

As you do the improvement actions you set for yourself, watch for and celebrate progress.

ACTIVITY MANAGEMENT SELF-ASSESSMENT

Please rate yourself from ... 1 = never ... to 7 = all the time.   ① ② ③ ④ ⑤ ⑥ ⑦

1 I am honest, responsible, and willing to do what it takes. I work hard. ○○○○○○○

2 I know what I value in life—in order of priority. ○○○○○○○

3 I can talk about my long-range goals (5 years) and why they motivate me. ○○○○○○○

4 I turned my survival and lifestyle needs into a monthly income goal. ○○○○○○○

5 I converted my monthly, lifestyle income goal into a sales goal. ○○○○○○○

6 It's important for me to reach my monthly sales goal. It's emotional to me. ○○○○○○○

7 My sales goal is converted into activity levels (prospects, appts., & quotes). ○○○○○○○

8 I manage a prospecting system with several lead development channels. ○○○○○○○

9 I network for leads with several groups or people according to a schedule. ○○○○○○○

10 I keep a prospect list and at any time can show it to someone. ○○○○○○○

11 I set and monitor a goal for prospects found each month. ○○○○○○○

12 I have enough prospects to call each week for the # of appointments I need. ○○○○○○○

13 I use some type of organizing system for my prospects, appointments, etc. ○○○○○○○

14 I know how (books, audio, practice, experience) to set 1st appointments. ○○○○○○○

15 I schedule phoning each week on my calendar as "calendared" time. ○○○○○○○

16 I monitor activity levels to meet targets for appointments set and held. ○○○○○○○

17 I set and monitor specific levels for # of quotes and the resulting sales. ○○○○○○○

18 I prioritize and do the most critical 'sales' activities each day. ○○○○○○○

19 I know my average $ of revenue per sale quoted AND sold. ○○○○○○○

20 I know my closing rate on the opportunities I get to quote. ○○○○○○○

21 I ask for referrals from each person who buys from me. ○○○○○○○

22 I weekly (or daily) forecast, on paper or in my mind, my sales progress. ○○○○○○○

23 I keep a sales board showing appointments, quotes, and sales levels. ○○○○○○○

24 I am willing to change my activities and their levels to help myself. ○○○○○○○

Totals — — — — — — —

Grand Total = _____ (out of 168)

Improvement Actions

_____
_____
_____
_____
_____
_____

Survival and Lifestyle Goal Setting (directions)

High-activity sales professionals run hard every day. Many do not stop long enough to understand their exact survival and lifestyle income needs. As a result, they unconsciously operate at survival levels just above or below what it takes to pay for the basic necessities of living. Very few think about lifestyle needs: debt reduction or eliminations, savings (for a rainy day), investments, education expenses for the kids, etc. As life continues, stuff just happens. Being unprepared, debt mounts and we experience bad forms of stress. Usually, this occurs because we have not done a good job at planning income and sales levels beyond survival.

So, let's change that. Let's change our mindset to lifestyle planning and activity levels. To begin this process, I've provided a *Survival and Lifestyle Goal Setting* tool. On the left, estimate your monthly needs for various income categories related to just staying even (survival). On the right, estimate what it will take to provide for a better lifestyle.

For both sides of your planning (survival and lifestyle), make sure to estimate these as monthly amounts of income. For survival numbers, this is easy to do. For lifestyle amounts, it is also easy when you create dates by which you will achieve a need. As an example, if you want to put 12,000 dollars in savings over the next year, then convert this number into 1,000 dollars of additional monthly income to be achieved. Add both sides together to arrive at your Lifestyle Goal.

Complete your goal setting by calculating your last six months average income and comparing that to your REAL (lifestyle) needs. Write down the EMOTIONAL impact of *selling at or below survival levels.* Then, write down your new target income and the EMOTIONAL impact of achieving a better lifestyle. Check a core motivation: progress, recognition, security, family, competition, duty, or personal achievement.

Setting Your Sales Goal

If you have a sales manager or leader, go to them to get help with converting your income goal into a sales goal and then into activity levels as shown in the book. Make conservative estimates as you do this. If you want help with this conversion, **SalesActivities.com** provides an activity wizard to help you. You may also email me, and I or one of my staff will help you as well.

Remember this. You are now operating at higher activity levels simply because you have needs that are perhaps greater than the company's sales budget for you, or simply because you are now wanting something more than you did before. That's great, and that's why I wrote the book. Go make things happen.

Sell BEYOND Survival,
Lance.

SURVIVAL AND LIFESTYLE GOAL SETTING TOOL

Name: _____   Date: _____

Survival Numbers (monthly)

Housing (rent or mortgage): _____
Utilities: _____
Food: _____
Telephone: _____
Gas: _____
Insurance: _____
Car Payment: _____
Credit Card Payments: _____
Loan Payments: _____
Other ( ): _____
Other ( ): _____
Survival Sub-Total: _____

A Better Lifestyle (monthly)

Debt reduction: _____
 (how much, by when, ÷ no. mos.)
House down payment: _____
 (how much, by when, ÷ no. mos.)
Savings: _____
 (how much, by when, ÷ no. mos.)
Car: _____
 (how much, by when, ÷ no. mos.)
Investment property: _____
 (how much, by when, ÷ no. mos.)
Other ( ): _____
 (how much, by when, ÷ no. mos.)
Other ( ): _____
 (how much, by when, ÷ no. mos.)

Lifestyle SubTotal: _____

Survival Sub-Total: _____

MONTHLY GRAND TOTAL: _____

Average income last six (6) months	IMPACT	Target income next six (6) months	IMPACT
_____		_____	
_____		_____	
_____		_____	
_____		_____	
_____		_____	
_____		_____	
average			

Check your primary motivation and write why it inspires you ...

❏ Progress _____

❏ Recognition _____

❏ Security _____

❏ Family _____

❏ Competition _____

❏ Duty _____

❏ Achievement _____

Remember this ...

If you have a sales manager or leader, go to them to get help with converting your income goal into a sales goal and then into activity levels as shown in the book. Make conservative estimates as you do this. If you want help with this conversion, SalesActivities.com provides an activity wizard to help you. You may also email me, and I or one of my staff will help you as well. Now, go get better. You can. Lance.